"Creating a Discipleship Cu

Creating a Discipleship Culture in Your Youth Ministry

"Moving beyond discipleship being one aspect of your youth ministry to creating a culture where making disciples is the centerpiece of everything you do."

By Rod Whitlock

To order additional copies go to RodWhitlock.com

Cover Design by Kyle Scheele (My wonderful Son-in-Law)

Dedicated to youth workers who tirelessly give of themselves to follow the mandate of Christ to make disciples. Your effort to reach students with the gospel and help them become life-long disciples does not go unnoticed. You may not be rewarded this side of Heaven, but God sees your heart and the many sacrifices you make to make disciples.

ENDORSEMENTS

(By students I had to privilege of making into disciples)

"I was new to faith and showed up as 15 year-old to church on Sunday by myself. I was a newbie and had lots of questions. Rod noticed me, took the time to talk to me, and invited me to the Wednesday night youth group. He showed interest in me by asking me to be around to help with various tasks at the church. Looking back I now know that it wasn't about the tasks, but rather about the time spent and the conversations. He showed up in "my world" by attending some of my soccer games and he came to my house once a week before school and we studied the Bible together. In a nutshell...Rod discipled me. I didn't just attend the youth group program. Rod invested in me as an individual. His approach wasn't fancy or complicated. It was real. It was caring. It was time. It was helpful and it has marked my life and ministry to this day."

-Eric Ferris, Executive Pastor, Vineyard Cincinnati

"Being available and fully present are two of the most impactful discipleship principles I saw modeled and made a difference in my life. Pastor Rod was willing to stop working and sought to understand me, to look past the initial question, to my heart. I never felt as though I was an inconvenience but rather a welcome guest. I am a different person as a result. I am a woman who is confident in my value to God and people. While not perfect, I do my best to notice others and truly listen. Rod took time out of his day to take notice of a young adult who pretended to have it all together. Without this I may not have ever understood that God cares for my every thought and sees me as valuable."

-Michelle Kaup, Wife, Mom and Graphic Designer

"Rod was one of my favorite leaders. He took our Masters Commission program to another level with his intentional development of our spiritual gifts and character. He met with our team on a regular basis, teaching and training us for ministry. I was able to travel with him during ministry experiences and see first hand his ministry to others. He gave me several opportunities to teach and lead worship, which helped me develop my own set of gifts. The one thing that will always stand out was how Rod held us accountable for our attitudes and the responsibilities he gave us. To this day I teach on this principle of discipleship. It continues to empower me as a leader today."

-Rev. Toby Schneckloth, Nebraska District Youth Director

"I came to know Jesus when I was a senior in high school, at a concert that Rod Whitlock invited me to. I then started attending the youth group led by Rod in Princeton, NJ. This youth group was **pivotal** in my learning, growing in Christ and forming friendships that I still have today. Rod and his wife, Kim, and the other leaders invested so much time in this group of teens; in addition to the weekly youth group meetings, they held one-on-one Bible studies, took us on camping trips, youth retreats, conventions, visited me where I worked…and so much more. They made you feel so valued by them and God. And the friendship between the leaders made you want to be around them. Mostly because of their investment in me, I am now a youth leader at my church."

-Christin Thompsen, Market Analyst, American Heart Association

"Rod was an outstanding youth pastor who also built a dream team of youth leaders by giving discipleship ministry away by way of delegation and multiplication. When I was in youth group, I had a very broken home, but a leader would come to my home and meet for breakfast weekly to do a Bible study and then take me to school. I learned Scripture, was prayed for, felt cared for and was loved. This created an environment for sanctification."

-David Hentschel, Pastor

"Rod knows what it takes to develop a mature reproducing disciple. I've known Rod for over 15 years and he has discipled me through many different stages and circumstances of life. He has consistently challenged me to grow stronger and more mature as a Christian, and given me wisdom and perspective, which has helped me, grow as a leader and a minister. Rod understands the importance of systematic and strategic discipleship, while still recognizing that everyone is at different levels of maturity and on different parts of the unique paths God has called each disciple to travel. He understands the importance of integrating theology, spiritual disciplines, and personal experiences into a holistic plan of intentional spiritual formation. When I met Rod 15 years ago, I was a fairly new Christian. Today, I am a chaplain on Active Duty in the Army. I'm not just leading religious services and counseling Soldiers, but fulfilling the great commission in all the things I do; Making disciples who make disciples, just like Rod taught me."

-Chaplain (Captain) John D. Ulrick, United States Army

"Pastor Rod was my youth pastor from the start of my middle school years through my freshman year. I was thankful to have him in my life to show me God's ways and to encourage me to be open to all God had planned for my life. Through his teachings and example I learned how to follow Jesus and that He loved me just as I am. Rod also taught me that I am fighting a spiritual battle – and how to be equipped for that battle with God's Word. He involved each of us in the group and built relationships with us. Even long after he left the impact on my life continues to this day."

-Angela (Daniels) Vanzino, Wife, Mother, Marketing Specialist & Compassionate Entrepreneur

"Reflecting on my experiences in Pastor Rod's youth group as a teenager, I recall a significant emphasis on discipleship. One valuable practice I've taken with me during those years and beyond was building relationships. These relationships helped to serve as role models or an accountability partners with others. Pastor Rod along with his wife, Kim as well as the other leaders, orchestrated opportunities to invest time in my life personally through speaking encouraging words while helping me in real life situations to grow in Christ."
    -Carrie Fisher O'Neill, Special Education Teacher

"Rod had an amazing and different role in my world – he was my Coach, my Youth Leader, my Pastor, and my friend, sometimes 2 or 3 of those roles at once! The discipleship process was woven together by him intentionally – he was an encouragement and inspiration to be like Christ – constantly reflecting Christ and Biblical wisdom. One distinguishing character about Rod is that no matter the position he held or the place he lived, he has always been touchable, approachable, honest, and transparent. Many days are marked by his input into my life, and I am better for it and grateful!"
    -Dan Lewiston, Pastor

"All the teachings that Rod gave were so very important to me as a follower. He was not only the one who disciple me but he was a friend. There was a time when I was going through a difficult period in my life. I turned to sex so as to find a man who would love me. I was lost. Rod and Kim continued to love me and help me find my way back to Jesus. His words and guidance came back to me when it came time to guide my own daughters as they encountered this vulnerable time in life."
    -Wished to remain anonymous

Contents

Section One-Discipleship

Section Two-Discipleshift

Section Three-Discipleshape

FOREWORD

DO YOU WANT TO BE AN ETERNAL GAME-CHANGER? If your answer to that question is "yes," then I think Rod Whitlock's book, *"Creating a Discipleship Culture in Your Youth Ministry,"* may be one of God's greatest answers in your life.

Statistics tell us that 92% of all individuals who come to Biblical faith in Christ do so ON OR BEFORE their 18th birthday. So if you're wanting to do something with your life that will help to create a spiritual "tipping point," discipling today's youth and young adult culture would be a tremendous "ground zero."

There's only one huge problem. TODAY'S CHURCH WORLD 'TALKS A GOOD GAME" IN DISCIPLESHIP…But often falls PAINFULLY SHORT in knowing how to create a true, practical CULTURE of discipleship. Honestly spoken, far more people "TALK" about discipleship than actually "LIVE IT." So that's where this excellent book can become such an invaluable resource to you.

Rod has held significant youth ministry leadership positions for over 30 years. A large portion of that time was spent leading an entire state of youth leaders and teenagers. Later, he went on to serve several years as a key youth ministry executive in a large and thriving national youth ministry where he focused on discipleship. But even more important, for many years he was also a local youth pastor. So from every possible angle, Rod has the practical experience and success to make this book a must-read.

People often ask me, after nearly 5 decades in full-time youth and young adult ministry, what I see as emerging trends. I can give several positive trends quickly. But sadly, there are a couple of patterns that deeply concern me. One of those is the fact that we are raising up lots of ministry LEADERS and CEO's in today's church world…but not nearly as many DISCIPLERS, SHEPHERDS, and true PASTORS. We're getting better at PROGRAMS…but worse at PEOPLE. And somehow, in my heart of hearts, I think that must break the heart of Jesus.

So grab a good cup of coffee and enjoy the "reading journey" that Rod has created for you. It might well be one of the most significant books you've read in many years. True discipleship is costly and often full of up's and down's. But if I am reading the New Testament accurately, it's Christ's only game plan for Kingdom transformation that LASTS.

In the Book of Acts, Christians were described by onlookers as "these are the men who have turned the world upside down!" THEY WERE NOT JUST CHRISTIANS...THEY WERE DISCIPLERS! So congratulations on the privilege of partnering with Christ to change a few people eternally in your corner of the world. Someday they may say of you, "This is someone who turned the world upside down."

Fondly Still Discipling One Person At A Time,

Jeanne Mayo

President, Youth Leader's Coach
Founder & Director of "The Cadre" mentorship journey
International youth & leadership communicator
Executive Director, Atlanta Leadership College
Director of Youth & Young Adult Ministries, Victory World Church, Norcross, Georgia

ACKNOWLEDGMENTS

As it is with any project there is always a great deal more to it than what one might initially see or read. Such is the case with this project. Much of the passion and genius behind this discipleship book is the result of key relationships I've enjoyed over the years. It goes without saying, but I am forever indebted for these relationships.

I want to begin by thanking my friend and best man in my wedding, Rich Williams. His tenacious invitations, during high school to attend youth group eventually led to my commitment to Christ. We remain good friends to this day and I shall always be grateful for his 'never-give-up' attitude. I also wish to thank my friend and eventual Lead Pastor, Gary Hoyt. Rich and Gary were instrumental in helping me become a disciple of Christ.

Much of who I am in Christ is a direct result of my youth pastor, Jeanne Mayo, and our youth group, SPIRENO (Spiritual Revolution Now). I heard many of her messages over the years, but it was her enthusiastic devotion to invest in me that shaped my life for Christ. I will never forget the many one on one conversations, weekly two-hour leadership meetings, Village Inn leader appointments, and weeklong retreats. There is only one person who loves people more than Jeanne. His name is Jesus.

I'm also indebted to the leaders and students of The ROCK (Radicals of Christ's Kingdom) for allowing me to privilege of discipling them. You taught me a great deal about being a follower and extended grace to me as I did my best to help you become life-long followers of Jesus.

I would be remiss to overlook my good friend and co-laborer in ministry, Jay Mooney.

His zeal to see students discipled in their faith is contagious. Much of what you read regarding the four connections – God, Family, Church and Cause has come as a result of Jay's vision, diligence and creativity. I am a richer man and better minister of the gospel because of Jay. I was challenged daily by his love for Jesus and excellence for ministry.

Thank you Abigail Turner for proofing and editing this work. Your edits, suggestions and feedback was deeply appreciated.

There is simply no way to adequately convey my gratitude to my wife, Kim and four children, Lindsay, Bethany, Michael and Christopher. They continue to love me amidst my flaws and graciously remind me that being a disciple begins in the home. I could not have asked for five greater people in my life.

I also wish to thank the thousands of leaders and students who allowed me to play a small part in their becoming followers of Christ. I am forever grateful for the grace you extended me.

It should go without saying, but I'll say it anyway. This book is a result of God's call and the salvation he purchased for me on the cross. I am joyfully and forever grateful to him for saving and calling me.

Rod Whitlock
Disciple of Jesus

INTRODUCTION

Your youth group has a culture. It may be by design or by default but truth be told, the way your group engages Christ, church, their campus and community is based on that culture.

Culture doesn't change overnight. It takes time to see the fruit of your labor in ministry and this is once again true when it comes to changing the culture of your ministry. Sadly, too many youth leaders leave for another youth group or ministry before seeing the change they set out to accomplish.

Here are a few thoughts for on creating culture for those leaders who plan on staying with a group and building a healthy youth ministry culture.

Healthy culture is far better than an unhealthy one. Create a healthy culture.

Honor the strengths of the current culture. Chances are you are not the first youth leader to lead this group. Others came before you doing their best to build a healthy culture, even if they didn't realize they were creating culture. Honor them and their efforts. This goes a long way with parents, leaders, and students and will help you build your own culture of youth ministry.

Don't fight the current culture; create more of the culture you want. Never criticize the existing culture; champion more of the culture you want to see. You won't change culture by criticizing it. Let your students hear you speak more on what you are for rather than on what you are against.

People carry the culture throughout the rest of the group. Look for and gather the most contagious individuals on your team and they will carry the desired culture to the rest of your group.

Match your strategy to the desired culture. Make sure that your team, programs, events, outings, messages, and behavior match the culture you are attempting to build. If it is your desire to build a culture of prayer in your group you will need to reinforce the culture of prayer in each activity.

For example: Pray for and with your team, hold prayer retreats, share messages on prayer, engage students in prayer, have a pre-service prayer option for leaders and students, and be a man or woman of prayer.

Don't try to convert people to your culture, convert them to follow Christ. Culture is secondary to our ultimate purpose of seeing people come to Christ and follow him as disciples. Ensure that students have an experience with Christ from the time they enter your youth room to the time they leave.

Focus on a few critical shifts - change is hard. One reason people find change difficult is that they are confused by it. When we attempt to change too many things at once we invite confusion.

So think small. Rather than attempt to change the entire group at once, start with your leaders. Create a culture within your team and let them slowly incorporate change into the lives of students.

Want your group to be more sacrificial? Start with your leadership team. Challenge them and provide opportunities for them to sacrifice. Over time they will echo your heart into the hearts of students they are discipling.

Develop proactive and reactive shifts. Perhaps you've heard what some companies and universities have done when determining where to place sidewalks?

Rather than put in a sidewalk during the building process, some companies waited for several months after the opening. They let the people determine the paths. As workers blazed paths from one building to another, they determined where the sidewalks should be placed.

Proactive shifts occur when you present a cultural shift and pour time and resources into making the change. Reactive shifts occur when those in your group, 'walk on the grass.' This allows you to use the momentum of the group to build culture.

Model the culture so that it can be translated to the family, campus, and community. Rather than being known as a taking youth ministry, be known as a loving, forgiving, serving, giving, and values oriented youth ministry. Encourage this behavior outside the walls of your youth group. Celebrate as you see students bringing hope to others outside of the church.

Tell, Tell, Tell your Story. When staff/leaders go home or are with friends, what stories do they tell about the youth ministry? The stories they tell, tell you what type of culture you've created. You want the stories they tell to be stories that reflect the culture you've created.

Tell your stories as you have opportunity to give announcements in church or have a platform in front of the church. Here are a few examples.

"Just wanted to let you know one of our students brought three of his friends to youth group this week and one of them gave their heart to Jesus."

"We had 15 students attend camp this last week and several rededicated their lives to Jesus."

"We've been praying for a student who needed healing. This week he went to the doctor and the doctor said he can find no evidence for additional treatment."

These quick sound bites change the culture of your youth ministry to a wider group. As you tell these stories others begin to tell these stories. You may not be able to give announcements, so use the platforms you currently have available.

Social media, a parent's eblast, short video clips sent out are all creative ways you can tell your story.

Rather than being the youth ministry that is constantly asking for resources from your church, be the group that is constantly giving, sharing, and serving your church, campus and community. Doing so will help you…

Create Culture

Below are the 31 cultural identities to help you create a discipleship culture in your youth ministry.

A Culture of Celebration
A Culture of Name Calling
A Culture of Cross Carriers
A Culture of Imitators
A Culture of Community
A Culture of Insurgents
A Culture of Expectation
A Culture of Frog Kissers
A Culture of Sending
A Culture of Learning, Loving, Leading
A Culture of Story-Telling
A Culture of Agents
A Culture of Sanctuary
A Culture of Growth Opportunities
A Culture of Gift Exchanges
A Culture of Servant Leadership
A Culture of Multiple Learning Experiences
A Culture of Redemptive Creativity
A Culture of Giving
A Culture of Unity
A Culture of Discernment
A Culture of Runners
A Culture of Identity
A Culture of Faith
A Culture of Compassion
A Culture of Praying Outside the Lines
A Culture of Reproducers
A Culture of Contributors

A Culture of Worship
A Culture of Family
A Culture of Discipleship

Your ultimate aim is not to create culture. Your desired outcome is to create disciples who change the culture of your youth ministry.

We've heard it before, "never confuse mission with method."

Mission always trumps method.

SECTION 1

"DISCIPLESHIP"

ONE

WHAT DID YOU CALL ME?

"Youth ministry is perfectly designed to achieve the results you are currently getting." -Andy Stanley

Do you know your youth ministry culture? Did you know you had one?

You should. It's vital to your future success in discipling students.

Your culture is shaped by the language, attitudes, experiences, behaviors, facility, and décor of your group. A youth group going to summer camp every year has a built in culture around this behavior.

The banners that hang in your youth room create culture. Youth worship nights just don't happen. Someone created this culture.

So how do I create culture?

> *Don't fight the current culture...create more of the culture you want.*

A great way to determine the current culture of your youth ministry is to ask students to tell their favorite story about the group. Upon arrival at my first youth pastorate, I continually heard stories of the great youth revival that took place a few years prior to my arrival. It seemed every story revolved around, 'the revival.'

Once you understand the current culture of your group, you'll need to decide if this is the culture you want to remain in your group. Be very careful about how you go about changing the culture if you decide to change it.

I've witnessed many groups that have experienced students leaving the ministry because of the vast amount of changes a new leader makes. I witnessed my share of the new youth leader coming in and cancelling events, programs, activities, and trips because the leader didn't want/like/believe in it. Change is hard, even for teens. So how do you change culture?

Don't fight the current culture…create more of the culture you want.

Rather than fight against something you don't like in your group, create more of what you do like. Avoid being the youth leader who stands up in front of the group telling them they don't pray enough. Be the leader who models it, encourages it, and provides opportunity for it. Celebrate answered prayer.

Create a Culture of Celebration

What you celebrate, you value. Celebrate often! Celebrating means students will have an easier time embracing change.

Some youth ministries may need to change their culture before attempting to make disciples. Attempting to make disciples in an unhealthy culture that is founded solely on entertainment, having a large youth ministry, or simply getting through another week, will prove difficult if not impossible.

The first disciples were fully engaged in becoming followers. So what was it that brought about their desire to follow? Perhaps it wasn't a 'what' as much as a 'who.' Those first followers had little idea of what they would be doing by saying yes to Jesus.

They didn't follow because of the tasks that would be asked of them so much as they followed because someone asked them to follow. In youth ministry we are that someone. I can hear some of you say that we are to get students to follow Jesus, not us. May I remind you that it was the Apostle Paul that challenged the followers at Corinth to follow him/his example as he followed Christ/the example of Christ.

It is both our responsibility and privilege to call students to a lifestyle of discipleship.

Matthew 4.19 – And he said to them, "Follow me, and I will make you become fishers of men." (ESV)

Jesus asked the disciples to follow him. I can't imagine the disciples had much of an idea of what that meant at this point. But what they did know was a leader with a message did the calling.

As a chosen leader, you too have a message. Don't be timid about calling individuals to follow. You have the greatest message anyone will ever hear. Call students with boldness and confidence to a life of following Christ.

Take a moment to write out your prayer to see students in your youth ministry following boldly after Jesus.

John 1.43 - The next day Jesus decided to go to Galilee. He found <u>Philip</u> and said to him, "Follow me." (ESV. Emphasis mine.)

Luke 5.27-28 - After this he went out and saw a tax collector named <u>Levi</u>, sitting at the tax booth. And he said to him, "Follow me." And leaving everything, he rose and followed him. (ESV. Emphasis mine.)

Two interesting observations are found in these verses. Jesus calls his followers <u>by name</u>. I've seen too many youth leaders stand on a stage challenging the crowd to follow. I want to challenge you as leaders to individually call your students by name.

"I'm asking you _____ (*Insert your name*) to please call your students, by name, to be part of the mission."

Walk up to the Brandon's and Katie's in your ministry, look them in the eye and ask them, by name, to follow.

I still remember the moment my youth leader did this in my life. As a matter of fact it wasn't a one-time call to follow. There were several times when my youth leader called me by name and challenged me to follow.

There were several times when other volunteer youth leaders pulled me aside, called me by name, and asked me to follow. Understand I'm not suggesting a formula in order to follow the call. What I am suggesting is that there is something deeply spiritual about calling someone by name to follow Christ.

There were many nights I spent as a teen and young adult at the altars of our youth ministry that I had a leader approach me to pray with me, challenge me, and listen.

One particular Wednesday I was feeling pretty discouraged and far from God. Another youth leader approached me (this was a part of our culture-people praying with/for each other) and asked what was going on. I shared for a few moments before Bob (I still remember this leader's name over 30 years later) told me to schedule an entire day with God.

He gave me some ideas and prayed with me. A few days later I did just what he asked. I spent 24 hours with God. I fasted, prayed, read, sang and listened. It was a turning point in my life.

Create a Name Calling Culture

Notice also in Luke 5.28, that Levi leaves everything, rises up, and follows. What is it you're offering students to get them to follow?

More than likely I'll receive some reactions to this, but offering a gift card or latest tech device for simply showing up to a service or event may not be the loudest message you want to send.

Appealing to the carnal nature of students is a breeding ground for carnal followers and creating an entitlement culture. I'm not opposed to special events and outreaches, but we must guard against creating a culture that simply rewards students for showing up.

I believe an entitlement culture is a deceptive tool of the enemy. We are one generation away from a world of people demanding someone to give them everything they ask for. This sets the stage for a world leader to then meet those needs, namely the antichrist.

Luke 9.57-62 says, "As they were going along the road, someone said to him, 'I will follow you wherever you go.' And Jesus said to him, 'Foxes have holes, and birds of the air have nests, but the Son of Man has nowhere to lay his head.' To another he said, 'Follow me.' But he said, 'Lord, let me first go and bury my father.' And Jesus said to him, 'Leave the dead to bury their own dead. But as for you, go and proclaim the kingdom of God.' Yet another said, 'I will follow you, Lord, but let me first say farewell to those at my home.' Jesus said to him, 'No one who puts his hand to the plow and looks back is fit for the kingdom of God.'" (ESV)

Following means being willing to give up everything for the cause of Christ.

Matthew 19.21 - Jesus said to him, "If you would be perfect, go, sell what you possess and give to the poor, and you will have treasure in heaven; and come, follow me." (ESV)

Which leads us to Matthew 10.

Matthew 10.38 – "And whoever does not take his cross and follow me is not worthy of me." (ESV)

Following means taking up their cross through the good and tough times.

Could it be one reason teens stop following, if they were following to begin with, is that we don't teach them about sacrifice and the call to embrace suffering? Our youth services are filled with statements such as, "God has a wonderful plan for your life."

At some point we owe it to followers to let them know that life may bring suffering, pain, offense, and persecution. Following Jesus is not always a honeymoon experience. During marriage a spouse gets sick or loses a job. A couple is unable to have a child or has a child that is physically or mentally challenged.

Yes, God has a wonderful plan, but sometimes pain redirects what we thought was his plan. Sometimes suffering detours our journey. Challenging students with the truth about life's difficulties, while equipping them to walk in greater faith, better prepares students for life.

Create a Culture of Cross Carriers

God's plan for our life doesn't change but sometimes life around us does. It's the follower who both understands this and learns how to walk through those difficult times that remains a committed follower. Consider a few examples from Scripture.

Abraham and Sarah struggled with barrenness even after receiving a promise from God.
David was chosen by God but spent years running from Saul.
Jacob was deceived and worked 14 years of his life for Laban before marrying Rachel.
Joseph received dreams from God only to spend years as a slave, be falsely accused and then thrown prison.
Moses spent 40 years in the desert.
Stephen was stoned to death.
Paul endured torture, imprisonment, and persecution.

Here we are taught that following Jesus is not a one-time decision.

John 10.27 – "My sheep hear my voice, and I know them, and they follow me." (ESV)

Notice Jesus alludes to the fact that his sheep (devoted followers) hear him and continue to follow. In other words, followers <u>continue</u> to hear his voice and <u>continue</u> to follow.

Following means a willingness to lay our life down for him.

John 13.36 - Simon Peter said to him, "Lord, where are you going?" Jesus answered him, "Where I am going you cannot follow me now, but you will follow afterward." (ESV)

There are times in our relationship with Jesus when we are not ready to fully follow him to the places he is going. Though we are not ready at this moment, we are always being prepared by Jesus to follow him, even to death. We see this call to in the following verses.

John 21.19 - (This he said to show by what kind of death he was to glorify God.) And after saying this he said to him, "Follow me." (ESV)

John 21.22 - Jesus said to him, "If it is my will that he remain until I come, what is that to you? You follow me!" (ESV)

Jesus calls the disciples to follow him, calling them by name (John 1.43).
They respond to Jesus' call and leave their current lifestyle (Luke 5.27-28).
They refused to give excuses why they couldn't follow (Luke 9.57-62).
They take up their cross (Matthew 10.38).
They continually listened for his voice and continue to follow (John 10.27).
They gave up the one thing that prevented them from following him (Matthew 19.21).
They are prepared to lay their lives down to follow (John 13.36).
They were to follow regardless of what others did (John 21.22).

Again, I'm not suggesting this as a formula to following Jesus. Rather, look at it as a process to following Jesus. Each day during our journey with Christ, we learn what it means to follow him beyond what we knew about following him. We are willing to take the next step in the journey.

Discipleship is a journey not a destination. Discipleship is an on-going process, not an outcome based matrix. It's not how many verses we've memorized or how many times we've read through the Bible or how much money we've given. Discipleship is about continuing to learn, love, and lead.

The problem with creating charts, graphs, or classes around becoming a disciple is that it implies there's a point in my walk with Christ that I've arrived as a follower. Once I've arrived I stop following and by definition, a follower continues to follow.

Want to create a culture of discipleship in your youth ministry?

Continually invite students by name.

Now that we've explored the importance of creating culture in your youth ministry, let's look at what a disciple is.

CULTURE SHAPING APPLICATION:

Write out your journey as a disciple.

Write out the name(s) of students you plan to call to follow Christ. Take time to pray for them by name.

Take a night to have students write out their journey with Christ. Have them turn these in for you and your leaders to read through. This will give you a better idea of where students are in their walk, how to pray for them and where to lead them next.

Pray for students by name to know an aspect of Jesus using names the Bible uses to describe him (page 34). One idea is to place the name of a student besides a characteristic of God. Pray that this student would understand this aspect of God. Another idea is to pray an attribute of God over your group using one name each day or week.

Almighty
Comforter
Compassionate
Counselor
Creator
Defender
Deliverer
Faithful
Father
Forgiving
Fortress
Friend
Generous
Giver
Gracious
Holy
Mighty
Omnipotent
Patient
Peace
Perfect
Powerful
Protector
Provider
Redeemer
Refuge
Rescuer
Restorer
Righteous
Savior
Servant
Shepherd
Shield
Teacher
Truth
Unfailing
Victorious
Warrior
Zealous

TWO

I'M HAVING A BABY!

The day our second child was born was one I'll never forget. From the first contraction my wife experienced, to our daughter's birth, was only three hours. Within seconds of being delivered our daughter stopped breathing. This was a result of the sudden change of the comfortable world she knew to a brand new world. Apparently her transition from the womb to the outside world occurred so fast that her body was unable to physically process the dramatic change.

Both her mom and I offered up intense prayers during those frantic moments in the hospital room that day. If it were not for those prayers and the first-rate training of the nurse, our daughter may not be here today. Thankfully, our daughter is not only with us today, but faithfully serving alongside her husband in youth ministry.

When a teenager responds to an invitation to receive Christ, we would do well to remember that they have just transitioned from a world they are all too familiar with, to a new world. Like my daughter, that transition may have been a quick one, requiring intense prayer and hands on training by a qualified individual.

This same principle is why we have a mandate to disciple students today: To help them transition from one world to another and to become devote followers in Christ and serve him with their lives.

The new birth into this new world demands we pray for and implement hands on care and training for the new follower.

This book is my attempt to encourage and equip you to do just this. It's my prayer that you will find practical concepts you can imitate to make life-long followers of Christ in your ministry.

"Salvation costs you nothing. Discipleship costs you everything."

Stop. Read that last statement again. Seriously.

We understand what a new convert looks like. We don't always recognize a disciple.

WHAT IS A DISCIPLE?

dis·ci·ple (dĭ-sī′pəl)
n.
a. One who embraces and assists in spreading the teachings of another.
b. An active adherent, as of a movement or philosophy.

There is a tremendous cost to creating a discipleship culture in your youth ministry. It will cost you everything. Are you ready to pay the price? Jesus modeled this principle by giving his very life in order to make disciples who would follow him and make more disciples.

Like Jesus, the disciples continued to show us this principle, as they too, gave everything.

As leaders in student ministry, we must be willing to do the same: give everything to making students into life-long disciples of Jesus.

> *There is a tremendous cost to creating a discipleship culture in your youth ministry.*

The early Church was birthed out of persecution. Do we truly believe that the Church that sees the return of Christ will experience anything less? We must prepare a generation that is more proficient at dealing with persecution than at attending pizzapaloozas. We can no longer afford to do youth ministry the same way we've approached it for years and expect to make an eternal difference in a world that is rapidly changing.

America is no longer the Christian nation it was once thought. Our students are dealing with an anti-God, anti-Church and anti-Religion culture out to destroy the gospel message. It's time we create a culture of discipleship in our youth ministries to prepare students for Last Day's ministry.

Why do we need a change of culture in our youth ministry? Allow me to give you a few reasons.

THE WORLD AROUND US IS CHANGING.

The culture around us has changed dramatically over the past few years. As a result, our teens are faced with issues that radically challenge their faith in monumental ways. We are witnessing an increase of persecution, the breakdown of biblical truth, and the demonstrative celebration of a blatant anti-God culture. This demands we re-examine the why and how of discipleship and radically shift our approach.

WE'VE FOCUSED OUR EFFORTS ON MAKING CONVERTS AT THE EXPENSE OF MAKING DISCIPLES.

For too long the Church has celebrated the new convert to Christianity while ignoring our mandate to make disciples. We are more zealous about someone coming to an altar than we are about disciple-makers bringing others to the altar. Yes, we should celebrate the new birth of a follower, but we must celebrate beyond the number of seats filled *in* our ministries to the number of students sent *from* our ministries. I'm not suggesting an either/or, converts OR disciples. Rather I'm emphasizing a both/and, disciples reaching others, who become disciples, who reach others.

WE ARE LOSING TEENS FOLLOWING GRADUATION.

We spend too much time debating over what percentage of teens are leaving our churches and/or faith in Christ following graduation and not enough time on the solution.

Whether 2% or 92% leave, it's far too many. Though we continue to lose teens, many groups continue to disciple students the way it's been done for several years. We must engage in methods that fulfill the mission and put a halt to the bleeding.

Making life-long followers will cost us everything but it is well worth it. If we want to see a world come to know Jesus, we must fulfill the Great Commission of *making* disciples. This is not new news to the devout follower, only news that needs to be renewed in our hearts and ministries.

Jesus said in Mark 1.17, "And Jesus said to them, 'Follow me, and I will *make* you become fishers of men.'" (ESV. Emphasis mine)

Making us into fishers of men is not automatic. It's a process. Jesus tells us he would have to *make* us into disciple makers.

WHAT'S YOUR SPIRITUAL DNA?

My guess as to why you're in youth ministry is because of your unbendable belief that students can change the world. Let's face it. Students are old enough to do something to change the world around them and still young enough to believe they can. You believe this too or you would not be reading this book and working with teens.

Ask yourself what your spiritual DNA looks like?

Most of us are fully aware that we have a physical DNA that makes up who we are. In the same way we also have a spiritual DNA that points to our purpose, passion, and mission in life. Read Psalms 139 and you'll discover that God created us in wonderful fashion.

Psalm 139.13-16 – "For you formed my inward parts;
you knitted me together in my mother's womb.
14 I praise you, for I am fearfully and wonderfully made.
Wonderful are your works;
my soul knows it very well.
15 My frame was not hidden from you,
when I was being made in secret,
intricately woven in the depths of the earth.
16 Your eyes saw my unformed substance;

> in your book were written, every one of them,
> the days that were formed for me,
> when as yet there was none of them." (ESV. Underline mine)

God intricately designed us during the several months we were in our mother's womb. Think about this for just a moment. We spent the first nine months of our lives in the presence of God the Father.

Our first life encounter was with the God who desperately wants relationship with us. The first thing we sensed in life was the presence of a loving and compassionate God.

You are I were not only fashioned in our mother's womb, but we were creatively constructed by the very hand of God for this exact moment in history. You are not an accident. How you got here is not nearly as crucial as what you do with the time you are here! Your arrival on this planet was no surprise to your Heavenly Father. Your parents may have been surprised but God was completely aware of and joyfully pleased with your arrival!

You were chosen before the creation of the world (Ephesians 1.4), with a heavenly calling for an earthly purpose. You were equipped with specific gifts of the Holy Spirit. You may have believed all along that you chose your calling, yet Scripture tells us God chose you.

The words, "…and who knows but that you have come to royal position for such a time as this," were not words reserved exclusively for queen Esther (Esther 4.14b). God breathes these words upon the life of every individual. We simply respond to his call.

It was while we were with him that he formed our inmost being. We were filled with his love, grace, compassion, strength and boldness. He formed our spiritual DNA, made up of the necessary ingredients to fulfill his call for our lives.

We are created in the image of a gracious Creator to be a reflection of who he is.

> We were beautifully formed in his presence.
> We were created with and for great purpose.
> We were put here at this exact time in history.
> We were given specific gifts to fulfill our call.
> We were fashioned to reflect Christ and his mission.

So to gain an idea of who we are and what we are called to do, we must look to God.

The first command God gave to Adam and Eve was to reproduce (Genesis 1.28). Thus woven within the fabric of our lives is the DNA to reproduce. Yes, I'm aware that this command from God to reproduce was a charge to reproduce physically. But don't overlook the greater meaning. Within the framework of our DNA is God's mandate to multiply.

Consider this.

One of the final commands Jesus gave us, prior to ascending to heaven was also to reproduce!

Matthew 28.19 – "Go therefore and *make* disciples of all nations, baptizing them in the name of the Father and of the Son and of the Holy Spirit,..." (ESV. Emphasis mine)

My DNA as a disciple maker became evident to me while serving in youth ministry over 30 years ago as a volunteer youth leader. I was working with a group of enthusiastic junior high students. It was during these early years of volunteer ministry that I taught a Jr. High Sunday School class of 30, ministered in a Sunday service format to over 120 junior highers, many of whom were bused in from low income housing, and led a Jr. High small group in our home each week. From there I served in a (K-12) Christian school as the Spiritual Life Director.

My call has also allowed me to serve as youth pastor, camp speaker, District Youth Director and, National Student Discipleship Director for my denomination. I say all of this to let you know that no matter my position, my personal delight in ministry has always revolved around the discipling of students and equipping of youth leaders to make more disciples.

Your call surpasses your position!

I still remember the first youth message I preached. Not too bad for my first one, but one horribly titled for a group of teenagers. The title of that first message was, 'Biblical Discipleship.' As bad as the title was, I so desperately wanted everyone to hear and understand the importance of being a disciple and then grasp the heart of Christ to disciple others.

Now 30 years later I am thoroughly convinced that the need to raise disciples is greater than ever before.

There are two primary reasons I believe understanding biblical discipleship is essential for each and every youth leader. First, we are commanded by God to go and make disciples (Matthew 28.19-20).

Second, every generation brings us closer to the return of Christ. I firmly believe that we have the privilege and responsibility to disciple a generation that will experience Christ's return or disciple the generation that will disciple the last generation. Regardless, each generation must be equipped to do a better job at making servant-leaders than the previous generation if the gospel is to advance.

The time is short, and we should live our lives and minister with this outlook. The writers of the New Testament firmly believed and lived with the return of Christ in mind. If they lived with his return in mind, we should all the more. As much as I love the activity and energy of youth ministry, I have never felt more of a need to truly disciple a generation than I do this current one.

Over the years I've come across complex charts and extensive outlines of what a disciple should look like. We've convoluted the picture to the point that no one really knows what a disciple is.

I've asked myself if there is a concise picture of a disciple to be found in Scripture? I believe one can best be captured here.

Ephesians 5.1-2, "Therefore be imitators of God, as beloved children. And walk in love, as Christ loved us and gave himself up for us, a fragrant offering and sacrifice to God." (ESV)

Paul gives us a list of sorts in Ephesians 4, outlining our new life as followers. We then come to chapter 5 where Paul starts with, 'Therefore...'

In other words, once we have new life we should (therefore) be imitators of God. And we are to be imitators as beloved children. We imitate out of an intimacy (beloved children). We walk in the love that Christ loved us with.

Disciples imitate God.

He loved, we love.
He sacrificed, we sacrifice.
He prayed, we pray.
He had compassion, we have compassion.
He served, we serve.
He taught truth, we teach truth.
He gave, we give.

We do what he did and what he is still doing today! Discipleship is not a destination but rather a journey. But I don't want to get ahead of myself. Let's continue.

We were created by a Creator to imitate our Creator's love, truth, forgiveness, kindness, justice, gentleness, joy, peace, goodness, mercy, and patience.

However, from the moment we are born we find ourselves entering a sinful world, filled with attributes contrary to those we were fashioned with while in the presence of God. We were born in sin and find ourselves in a spiritual war, in a fight to retain the image of our Creator.

Imagine a newborn baby trying to take care of himself. It would be impossible for the newborn to feed and clean himself. Over time the newborn baby would become sick and die.

The task for caring for a newborn falls into the hands of his parents. During this process of growth, the parents care for the child giving every chance for a growing, healthy existence.

In like manner, when a student is born again, they need a 'parent' to feed and teach them how to live in this new world. We are called to restore the new follower back into the design of their Creator.

"Discipleship is a process of restoring an individual back to God's original design and purpose."

What purpose? "To be imitators of God."

Growing up with three brothers and sisters meant there was always one of us attempting to get at one of the other siblings. The weapon of choice among us often came in the form of imitating the sayings or movements of one of the other siblings. Whether it was copying their actions or what they said, it seemed this one act was the most torturous of all.

"Stop copying me!"

"Mom, (insert name of sibling here) won't stop imitating me!"

"Copy cat, dirty rat!"

I find it interesting that within our very nature is the desire to imitate. We find this imitation game in each of our students.

We witness how they imitate the dress, talk, actions, etc... of celebrities and athletes they follow. What if we could get our students to go beyond simply saying they follow Jesus, but to imitate him?

I had the opportunity to speak at a regional youth retreat a few years back. There were about six youth groups represented, each with a youth leader and several students. I still remember that first night as we responded to God at the altar.

As the worship band played, there was a youth leader and his group sitting in the pews of the church, with their Bibles open, each one reading from it. Another group kneeling as they pounded the altars and passionately shouted for more of God in their lives.

To my left was a leader standing with his group, with arms raised softly singing in worship. Still another leader and group quietly sitting as they reflected on the message. What caught my attention was the fact that each group of students was imitating their leader's response to God.

Create a Culture of Imitators.

3 John 11 – "Dear friend, do not imitate what is evil but what is good. Anyone who does what is good is from God. Anyone who does what is evil has not seen God." (NIV)

Before moving on, let's take some time to reflect on what we've just read.

CULTURE SHAPING QUESTIONS:

Define 'Disciple' in your own words.

Write out your spiritual DNA? (Your gifts, calling, passions, purpose)

What are ways we are to imitate God?

What are some ways teens in your youth ministry are currently imitating God?

What are additional areas you'd like to see teens in your ministry imitate God?

What steps do you have in place to help a teen transition when they receive Christ in your youth ministry?

THREE

PICK ME!

Most of us remember the feeling we had standing against the backstop, waiting to be picked by one of the two team captains, for a game of kickball. With each pick, in which we weren't chosen, panic set in as we realized the reality of being picked last or not at all, was a real possibility. So it is when we come to a verse such as John 15.16, memories of not being chosen leave us less confident in God's choice of us.

The meaning of the phrase, 'I chose you' is interesting. When you consider the meaning of the original text it carries the idea of, 'I chose you and give to you the ability to respond to that call.' Jesus' choice of us came with the ability to respond to his choice. It was not out of an obligation. He chose us when we offered nothing to him in return.

One might say it like this.

"I choose you to be on my kickball team and give you the ability to kick the ball."

During the days that Jesus walked the earth, students of Rabbis would ask the Rabbi for permission to follow and become his disciple. Jesus turned this concept around when he asked the disciples to follow him. In other words, individuals who previously were overlooked were asked to follow him. He did not wait for you to ask, he chose you!

John 15.16 – "You did not choose me, but I chose you and appointed you that you should go and bear fruit and that your fruit should abide, so that whatever you ask the Father in my name, he may give it to you." (ESV. Underline mine.)

Part of your initial encounter with God was being chosen by him to make disciples. Not only were you chosen but you were appointed to go and bear fruit. But not just bear fruit – fruit that lasts!

Perhaps you've thought all along that you chose student ministry. In reality, God chose you! Your ministry to teens is not a mistaken call. It is a deliberate commission from God, himself.

I love the last part of verse 16, "so whatever you ask the Father in my name, he may give it to you."

As we make disciples, God gives us what we ask. I believe he does this because he wants us to have everything we need to make more disciples. Additionally, he knows we will ask for things that help us fulfill this mission, to make more disciples.

> He chose you.
> He appointed you.
> He asks you to bear lasting fruit.
> He gives you what you need...

WHY?

...to make disciples.

I've had the wonderful privilege of living this verse first hand. While serving in New Jersey as a new youth pastor I meet with various male students each morning in their homes to disciple them. My schedule looked something like this. I would meet with Terry on Tuesday, John on Wednesday, Mark on Thursday and Eric on Friday. We would meet from 6.30 to about 7.30.

I spent the first half-hour meeting in their home for Bible study, prayer and to talk about life issues they were facing. During the next half-hour I would drive them to school. Upon reaching the campus we would sit in my car and pray for the teachers and students on the campus.

As a result of meeting with students, I was able to share moments with parents and siblings of each of the young men. This opened many doors for me during the year. I was able to see whole families come to Christ and begin attending our church.

I was invited to conduct weddings and minister at funerals of family members I had previously never met and would not have met had I not been in their house each week. All because I took time to meet and disciple their son. I had parents offering their homes and giving resources to our youth ministry as a result.

The model of how you create this culture is not what's important here. What is important is the mission. WHEN you choose to disciple is not nearly as important as the WHY and HOW.

"So that whatever you ask the Father in my name, he may give it to you."

To change the culture of your youth ministry you need to be calculated. You cannot disciple the crowd; discipleship takes place as you are part of a community.

Create a Culture of Community

Two of the four young men lived in single parent homes. One might say I became their father through the gospel.

1 Corinthians 4.15 – "For even if you had ten thousand others to teach you about Christ, you have only one spiritual father. For I became your father in Christ Jesus when I preached the Good News to you." (NLT)

More and more teens are growing up in non-traditional homes. (I address this in a later chapter.) As a result we need youth ministries that create a culture of community. Over the years I've had teens refer to me and call me, dad. I don't say this to bring attention to myself. Rather, I mention it to bring attention to the need of students to have spiritual parents who genuinely care for them.

1 Thessalonians 2.11-12 – "And you know that we treated each of you as a father treats his own children. We pleaded with you, encouraged you, and urged you to live your lives in a way that God would consider worthy. For he called you to share in his Kingdom and glory." (NLT)

I'm not in any way suggesting that we take the place of mom and/or dad. As you will read later we should make it a priority to connect with a student's parents, as I did each week while meeting with one of the students. What I am advocating is creating a culture where students know they are loved and are safe.

Kate was not someone you would choose for your team. She appeared alone one night in our youth ministry. Although a junior by age, she was much younger developmentally and emotionally. Kate didn't talk much. She only answered questions if she was asked directly.

Over time we earned her trust and, although she seldom participated in activities, she showed up for most every event. Our leaders loved on her and made every effort to include her on the team. As a result her parents became huge fans of our youth ministry. They offered their home to us for events and became advocates for our ministry.

Make disciples…that last…and he gives us what we need.

I once heard a pastor friend of mine say, "if it's good enough for Jesus, it's good enough for me."

Jesus not only asked us to make disciples, but he spent his days of ministry discipling his followers. He could have spent all of his time serving others but he spent much of his time training up young men to continue the mission of serving others. Jesus knew by investing time in the lives of the disciples he would multiply his reach.

Our call is no different today. My ministry IS making disciples. We are staging a generation of students to fight a war they have never fought.

We are staging a generation of students to fight a spiritual war they have never fought. Perhaps a war that no other generation has ever fought.

No, that was not a misprint. I meant to write it out twice so you would read it again. It's that important.

The longer we create disciples who view Christianity as an individual accomplishment we miss the mission of Jesus. Read through Scripture and you'll see that Jesus always seemed to have at least a few disciples with him. Even when Jesus sent the disciples out, they walked with one another in community and mission.

I came across this article a while back and believe it to be a prophetic word for youth ministers, youth ministries and students.

You Are A Dangerous Generation
by Melody Green

Have you ever seen a movie where people keep trying to kill someone... only that person doesn't realize someone is after them? Strange things keep happening. Near misses, so-called accidents, explosions they barely escape, etc. The audience knows what's going on. They keep anxiously hoping that person will realize someone is trying to take them out. That they are a target.

But it takes this "target" over half the movie to figure it out. When they finally do, they start fighting back. Getting smart. Avoiding danger. Dodging bullets. Planning counter attacks. Winning.

But even after they figure out they're a target, it's usually near the end of the movie before they can figure out WHY someone is after them. WHY they are a target. Finally they realize it's something they have, or know... or perhaps just who they are... that makes them so important to destroy.

So it is with your generation.

Sometimes you have to recognize the intensity of the enemy's attack before you understand just how much of a threat your are... how dangerous you are.

Your generation is a big threat to the enemy. Why? Because you have a huge call on your lives. A big, intense anointing that God is going to lay on you once you realize WHO you are in Him. You are like no other generation before you. It is the last days anointing—of healing the sick, raising the dead, and seeing multitudes come into the Kingdom through your witness and ministry. There is a powerful call on your whole generation.

That is why the enemy wants to take you out. That is why he has laid so many traps for you. [1]

The students we love on are a genuine threat to the enemy and his plans. We must be serious about making disciples who can recognize and biblically respond to the schemes of the enemy.

Create a Culture of Insurgents

Create a culture where students are encouraged and equipped to revolt against the status quo, who understand the times in which they live. Students who realize the God ordained destiny on their lives. Students who truly wish to make a difference.

We make disciples by proclaiming the truth about Jesus. Let's remember that John 14.6 tells us Jesus IS the Way, the Truth and the Life. In other words, we make disciples by proclaiming the TRUTH about the Way, the Truth and the Life.

Don't limit your ministry to telling students the way to Jesus; compel them to know THE Way. We aren't to simply teach others about what is true, we convince them to embrace THE Truth.

> *Discipleship is not microwaveable.*

We shouldn't stop at sharing with students how to do life; we need to challenge them to live close to THE Life.

Isn't this what Jesus did with his disciples? It appears Jesus was far more interested in showing his disciples who he was, rather than what he could do. To use an old saying, "things are better caught

1(http://www.lastdaysministries.org/Articles/1000008656/Last_Days_Ministries/LDM/Discipleship_Teachings/Melody_Green/You_Are_A.aspx)

than taught." Jesus understood that by spending time with his disciples they would catch his heart for God and people.

By spending time with Jesus the disciples were able to hear the very heartbeat of Jesus as they learned from him. As corny as it sounds I wonder if the disciples ever approached a new town and asked each other, "what would Jesus do?"

Discipleship is not microwaveable. Discipling students is more like cooking with a crockpot. Even Jesus needed three years to bring the disciples to a place where he could fully release them into ministry.

When is a good time to disciple?

Here are a few suggestions:

Saturday morning meeting at your favorite coffee stop. In addition to teens having a cell phone, teens also have their favorite coffee concoction. My favorite is an iced coffee with white mocha syrup!

Make these times informal and with a small group of students. Allow for questions, interaction and honest questions about the faith.

Meet prior to school. I did this as a youth leader, as I mentioned earlier. This allowed me to meet with four different students each week, each semester.

If you're a stay at home mom, why not invite a few girls over after school, for an evening or on a Saturday? Together you can make cookies, take care of the babies, or make a special meal. Take a few moments during this time to pray for each other, read through a chapter and talk about matters the students are dealing with.

Titus 2.1-5 "You must teach what is in accord with sound doctrine. Teach the older men to be temperate, worthy of respect, self-controlled, and sound in faith, in love and in endurance. Likewise, teach the older women to be reverent in the way they live, not to be slanderers or addicted to much wine, but to teach what is good. <u>Then they can train the younger women</u> to love their husbands and children, to be self-controlled and pure, to be busy at home, to be kind, and to be subject to their husbands, so that no one will malign the word of God." (NIV. Underline mine.)

Life is crazy busy. The fact is many of us are crunched for time. For us to add, to our already busy schedule, a meeting with students can become an exercise in futility. One idea is to grab one or two students as you're running errands.

Rather than head out alone, plan it so you can swing by a couple of student's home and take them with you. This gives you opportunity to interact with them while driving. It also affords teaching moments as you interact with people outside the church. These are valuable teaching moments. Jesus did this a great deal with His own disciples.

There are many accounts when Jesus would take a moment to impart into the lives of the disciples as they simply did life.

Meet for lunch with other youth leaders. They need to be discipled as a follower also.

Without a doubt, one of our primary responsibilities as youth leaders is to train up additional leaders for ministry. The role of developing student leaders is not limited to when students become adults and graduate from our youth ministries, but it includes shaping leaders for the present.

By expanding our leadership through the lives of student leaders, we are multiplying our efforts, thus increasing our influence in the lives of more students. Our student leaders become ambassadors of Christ and of our youth ministry.

CULTURE SHAPING QUESTIONS:

How does knowing that Jesus chose, appointed and gave you resources give you confidence to make disciples?

Who are 2-3 students you could begin discipling today?

How could you rearrange your schedule in order to give more time to discipling students?

Make a list of things you need in your youth ministry that will help you make disciples. Take some time and ask Jesus to provide these things.

FOUR

NINJA WARRIOR STUFF

Ever watch individuals attempt to go through those staggering obstacles on, American Ninja Warrior? Only a few can make it all the way to the end and it generally boils down to a few carefully timed moves.

Changing your culture operates in much the same way. You may see the finish line but to get there you need to make your way through some pretty arduous obstacles.

As I've traveled throughout the country meeting with youth leaders committed to reaching students, I'm continually faced with this one recurring question: Whether I'm in California or New Jersey, Florida or Alaska, youth leaders want to know how to effectively disciple their teens.

The simple answer is to begin by creating a culture of discipleship. Although the answer is easy, implementing the solution requires much more work. Over the next two chapters I'll give several challenges to creating a discipleship culture.

Consider discussing each one with your team over the next several months. Make time to come up with some solutions and possible answers to each one.

We Are In a Spiritual War

Don't forget that our struggle is not that hyperactive eighth grade boy running around causing problems for every youth leader.

Though it may seem this is our fight, our fight is a spiritual one. As much as I love the lights, smoke machine, screens and energetic worship band, let's remember that at the core of our call is equipping a teen to go into his or her world and make more disciples.

We are supernatural beings, living in a supernatural world, serving a supernatural God for a supernatural purpose, with a supernatural enemy. Let's remember, we are a soul with a body. We are not a body (although we have one) we are an eternal soul.

Our students are in a spiritual war. An enemy bent on taking down their family, your ministry and all of our souls.

Stop reading for just a moment and pray. I'll wait.

> *We are in a spiritual war. We fight with spiritual weapons.*

Thanks for taking a moment to pray for your students.

She was a petite, full of life and energy freshman in our youth ministry. Becky was so excited about reaching students on her campus and desperately wanted to start a Bible club. Her enthusiasm was quickly met with the realities of this spiritual battle her first week on campus.

She came to me on the first youth meeting night following the first day of school.

"Pastor Rod. I asked my principal permission to start a Bible club on campus and she said no."

To say that Becky was disappointed would be a huge understatement. I encouraged her and challenged her to pray that God would open doors.

Later I spoke with Bruce, one of my youth leaders, and asked if he would be willing to meet with me once a week on Becky's campus to pray for open doors. He agreed and so each Wednesday morning prior to the start of school, we met at the campus for one purpose.

We met to pray for a change in the culture.

Most days we walked around the campus praying that the walls of opposition would be torn down. On the days when the weather was bad we simply prayed in the car.

We prayed that the administration and teachers would welcome a Bible club on campus. We prayed that Becky would be able to start that Bible club.

We did this for the entire school year.

And so it was that on the first youth meeting night following the first day of school for Becky's sophomore year, that petite, energetic young girl enthusiastically bounced her way to me.

"Pastor Rod," She said. "You'll never guess what happened over the summer!"

Becky went on to tell me that over the summer the entire administration had left the high school and a new administration had been put in place.

She then proceeded to tell me that she approached the new principal the first day and asked if she could have a Bible club on campus. The new principal said yes to her request and told her that if she needed a club sponsor, that he would be the Club's sponsor!

The only thing that changed during the year? We prayed!

We are in a spiritual war. We fight with spiritual weapons. We anticipate spiritual victories!

Create a Culture of Expectation

Never underestimate the power of prayer! Expect to win!

Lack of Parent's Involvement

Most youth ministries I've encountered are doing good to have 50% of parents attend the church on Sundays. Many teens are coming to youth groups on their own or with a friend and their parents either don't know about the group, don't care, or are simply happy their teenager isn't doing drugs or alcohol.

I'm convinced that getting parents on board is vital to the success of raising healthy disciples. The more reinforcement you as a youth leader have in the home the better chance a teen remains a follower. It's when a student hears one message at church and one at home that confusion sets in for your students.

I didn't become a follower until my junior year in high school. I was raised in a non-Christian, non-church going home. I remember coming home after attending the youth group and realize I could have a relationship with God, only to return home and told I had to stop going to that church.

It was very puzzling for me as a young man who wanted to please my parents and yet knew there was something special about the church. There are some students in your youth ministry who don't come every week to your youth ministry because they are conflicted by what they encounter at church and what they experience at home.

You'll find some suggestions on how to connect with parents later.

A Generation of Orphans

For the first time in the history of our nation, less than 50% of families are comprised of the traditional mom and dad. Additionally, as I write this book, 64% of women under age 30 are having at least one baby out of wedlock.[1] The rate is as high as 72% for African Americans.[2]

This challenge is not going to get any better either. It is believed that more children will grow up in non-traditional homes. This has far

[1](http://www.slate.com/articles/business/moneybox/2014/06/for_millennials_out_of_wedlock_chil dbirth_is_the_norm_now_what.html)
[2](http://www.politifact.com/truth-o-meter/statements/2013/jul/29/don-lemon/cnns-don-lemon-says-more-72-percent-african-americ/)

reaching implications for the youth leader. As these students attend our youth ministries we are faced with helping them grasp the idea of a loving heavenly Father who is present in their lives.

Combine this with students who are constantly being relocated to foster homes or who have never met one or both parents and the face of youth ministry changes dramatically.

I understand the implications of this first-hand.

I told you I grew up in a non-Christian home. I also grew up having had four fathers over the course of my life. Being born out of wedlock, multiple divorces, single parenting, constant moving, and adoption was my reality. Without going into the detail of this, I can tell you that had a tremendous impact on my spiritual development over the years.

My first youth pastor was a woman named Jeanne Mayo. I tell you this for three reasons. First, I look back and see the hand of God on my life. You see, I grew up not trusting men. Knowing this, God put me in a youth ministry with a woman leader who became my spiritual mom. She remains a spiritual parent to me to this day.

The second reason I mention this is to encourage the women youth leaders reading this book. You simply have no idea how your life and the fact that you're a woman impacts the students in your ministry. Be encouraged! Don't listen to the lies of the enemy that simply because you're a woman you can't be a tremendous youth leader. I am eternally grateful for women who take up the call of youth ministry.

Finally, the one reason Jeanne has so many spiritual sons and daughters (disciples) is because she has spent her life showing leaders and students who Jesus is. She made following Jesus meaningful and fun! As I've often heard her say and more importantly seen in her life, be Jesus with skin on. She was and remains that to so many today!

Ministry to students who are in foster care and/or adopted can be a challenging one. Lack of trust, fear, inability to show love, internal pain, depression, etc…are just a few of the feelings students from broken homes may exhibit. Never give up loving these students to Jesus.

As my youth pastor, Jeanne Mayo, would often say, "Be a frog kisser." In other words…

Create A Culture of Frog Kissers

Every student in your youth ministry is a prince or princess but may not know it. They just need to be kissed. Create a culture of genuine encouragement.

Leaderless Youth Ministries

Jesus had 12 followers. Pretty ambitious. Even the most seasoned youth minister can only truly disciple 8-12 teens and I would argue that eight is the maximum in order to be effective. This being the case it means that if your youth ministry is made up of 30 students, you will need at least four leaders who know how to disciple teens.

Did you catch that?

Not just youth leaders…but youth leaders who know how to disciple.

How many students do you want to reach? 50? 100? Whatever the number, divide that by eight. This is the number of leaders you will need to disciple to make disciples. Thus, as a leader it becomes a priority to recruit and train more leaders. I would argue that the most important role of the youth leader is not to reach students.

I would maintain that your three most vital culture-changing roles are to…

1. Bridge the Gap Between the Youth Ministry and Church.
2. Help Connect Parents
3. Raise Leaders

Let's look at your first role of bridging the gap between your youth ministry and the church.

Why? No one else in your church is doing this.

This is fundamental to a healthy culture of youth ministry in your church. You don't want students leaving the church following graduation. One reason some do is because they've never really connected with the adult congregation.

Helping the generations appreciate and respect each other ensures a greater chance of current students becoming future leaders in the church. Brag on your students to the adults in your church and train up your students on how to respect and value the adult followers.

Coordinate opportunities for adults and teens to interact in positive ways.

Here are a few thoughts:

Following a service, have the youth host a Sunday Sundae. Invite adults to build and enjoy free ice cream sundaes. Have the teens welcome and help serve the adults.

Hold a free car wash and invite the adults to attend. This can be a part of a community car wash for donations but adults from your church get a free wash.

Teens act as parking lot greeters and escort adults under an umbrella during raining weather.

Have junior high students serve by parking cars for the adults. (Ha! Just wanted to make sure you are paying attention.)

2. Help Connect Parents.

Have you noticed there are more books on leadership than on parenting? Probably because helping someone become a leader is easier than becoming a good parent and let's face it, being a good parent isn't as sexy as being a good leader.

Showing parents that you genuinely care about them and their family leaves an indelible mark on them. I give several ideas at the end of this book on how you can do this but allow me to share one idea that greatly sent this message to parents.

We held POT Parties (Parents Of Teens-not what you were thinking, was it)? occasionally to encourage and equip our parents. We invited all our parents and met in a location other than the church, such as the local high school or library. By meeting in these locations rather than the church it lowered the defenses of the parents who didn't attend our church.

We served refreshments, had some fun activities and kept the meeting to an hour. Of course we stayed and talked with parents until the last one left.

Most youth leaders may struggle with teaching parents of teens how to parent teens because they themselves are younger and have never had a teenager in the home. This was the case for me. My oldest child was only five years old when we developed these meetings.

How was I going to equip parents on raising a teenager? Fortunately I was smart enough to realize I wasn't. I found video teachings, books and articles, and asked parents of teens from the church to teach. These parents had solid homes and were able to communicate truths to help other parents.

3. Raise Leaders.

I'll say it again. In order to effectively disciple teens you need empowered leaders. Training more leaders to disciple means more students can be discipled and become student-leaders. As students are discipled they take on the role of reaching and discipling others.

Most students who come to your youth ministry are not going to come because you invited them. Most are going to come because another student invited them.

One of the greatest observations I made as a student and later as a leader in my youth group was watching leaders be sent out to minister in other locations. Leaders weren't just made leaders to lead the group I was a part of. There was a culture of 'sending.'

Create a Culture of Sending

I watched as leaders in our youth ministry were sent out as missionaries, pastors, evangelists, worship pastors, youth leaders of other groups, para-church leaders and leaders in other churches. What was even more fascinating was that each time a leader was sent, a new leader within our group would emerge.

It seemed the more we sent, the more we saw take on the mantle of leadership.

> *In order to effectively disciple teens you need empowered leaders.*

Recall the story found in 2 Kings 4? Elisha tells the widow woman to collect as many jars as possible. As long as she had jars she had oil flowing. Once there were no more jars the oil stopped.

As long as we gather leaders around us, the oil continues to flow. The issue is not the supply of God. He is enough. The issue is gathering enough leaders for God to fill.

Changing culture requires large quantities of oil. Large quantities of oil come from having several vessels to fill. Creating a sending culture keeps us ever mindful that the leaders ultimately belong to God and not us or our ministry. It's the unselfish leader who God can use to advance his Kingdom.

Let's look at a few more challenges in the next chapter.

FIVE

NINJA WARRIOR STUFF

We Really Don't Know What a Disciple Looks Like

So what exactly does it mean to be a disciple? Is a disciple someone who does a bunch of spiritual things or someone who acts a certain way or someone who graduates from a class on discipleship? If we use our Scriptural definition of someone who imitates and does what God is doing (Ephesians 5.1), then how do we get a student to that point and what does it look like?

Perhaps part of the problem for us is that we think of a disciple as someone who has accomplished a certain set of standards or passed a number of tests. Perhaps we should change our thinking. Rather than think of someone as having arrived (destination) at becoming a disciple, we should think of a disciple as someone who is doing (journey) what God is doing. Rather than viewing discipleship as a finished product, think of it as an ongoing process of following Jesus.

John 6.66 – "After this many of his disciples turned back and no longer walked with him." (ESV)

Following one of Jesus' teachings on who he was, some of his disciples left him. They left because the teaching was too hard for them. Note a couple of things from John 6.66,

"Many of his disciples left."

There may be times when we experience individuals leaving our youth ministry as we challenge them to follow. We shouldn't be afraid to speak truth out of fear of losing some.

"His disciples."

These followers *were* disciples. They were walking with him at the time. No one ever arrives at being a disciple. Disciples continue to

---

walk with Jesus or leave him. We can't assume that just because someone is called a disciple, they will always be a disciple. Sadly, some will turn away.

"No longer walked with him."

They stopped following. This tells us that being a disciple is exemplified by walking with Jesus. Again, using our definition, doing what Jesus did and is doing…walking WITH him.

Even after completing three years of hands on ministry with Jesus the disciples still had much to learn. Yes they were called disciples, but they continued to grow as disciples. What changed was they went from primarily <u>learning</u> from Jesus, to <u>loving</u> others, and then <u>leading</u> others to a relationship with Christ, who would now begin the learning process.

Create a Culture of Learning, Loving, Leading

Increase in Mental/Physical Health Issues in Students

Let me start off by saying that I'm not a doctor or pharmacist, yet without a doubt students today take more medication than when I was a teenager. Students are diagnosed with conditions that didn't exist a few years ago. I'm reminded of this with each camp I attend and watch students line up to receive their daily medication.

Teens today are the most medicated and addicted generation in history. Additionally, more teens are obese or overweight than any other time in history. These issues afford unique challenges in making passionate disciples.

Youth leaders are faced with a youth room filled with students who are diagnosed with mental and physical ailments. Most leaders don't understand the underlying need for the medication and/or aren't equipped to handle behaviors necessitating the medication or as a result of the medication.

Very little guidance is available to the youth leader on where to turn or what help there is in order to reach and then disciple a student struggling with diagnoses or treatments they are currently under from a medical professional.

Perhaps looking for help from a qualified individual, in your church, who has a working knowledge of some of these issues would be of value. Books or articles can also help. At the very least it's a good starting place.

At the very least you'll want to begin by sitting down with the parents to ask them how your youth ministry can best minister to their son or daughter. Take time to listen to students who are struggling and engage in conversations with a school counselor or other professional for help.

Youth Culture is Fast-Paced and Ever Evolving

Just about the time the groovy, dope, awesome, bodacious, cool youth leader gets his/her head around the dress, music, apps, movies, entertainment, language, etc…it changes! Just try showing a video to illustrate your message and watch how many students turn to their friends to tell them they've already seen it. The Internet has not only changed how students get their information but the speed at which they get it.

Occasionally I'll get with a group of students and ask them to teach me. Think of it as reverse mentoring, the younger teaching the older. I'll ask them about words, apps, music, etc. Most students are engaged with today's culture and happy to tell me. This keeps me up to speed and gives students the opportunity to discuss things they are confident about.

Let me take some pressure off of you. Don't feel you need to keep up with everything in a teen's world. Most teens understand that you're an old adult and no longer hip (can I still use that word?).

They're pretty forgiving on this one. Never underestimate the power of listening. You'll be surprised how much you can learn simply by listening to teens talk in informal settings.

Youth Ministry Seems to Get Criticized More Than Other Ministries

It appears that more books are written on how bad a job youth ministry or the youth minister is doing than on equipping youth leaders to strategically reach and disciple teens. Whether true or not, it seems that a new stat, book or article comes out criticizing the heroic efforts of youth leaders on a regular basis.

The hard working youth leader continually hears how many teens are leaving the Church following graduation, suggesting they are doing a poor job. I believe that even if one leaves, it's one too many. Jesus states this in the parable of the lost sheep (Luke 15.4).

Yet to suggest that 80% or 90% of teens are leaving the Church following graduation is irresponsible reporting and has hidden motives.

We need youth leaders who are devoted followers of Jesus now more than ever. Consider the several examples in Scripture of young men and women who were called to do great things. Joseph, David, Daniel, Esther, Mary, and the disciples are just a few examples of individuals called in what we would refer to as their teen years.

I understand that the time of Daniel, for example, was a different time than the time than we live in today. Yet I remain in awe of the countless stories of students who sense a call from God to ministry while in their teen years.

At the same time I can count on one hand how many adults shared how they sensed a call from God to ministry during their adult years. Teens not only have the ability to hear from God, but believe they can make a difference, and are able to begin the preparation to answer the call.

Think of how many revolutions over the course of history have begun with a teenager at the helm. Even today we read of students who are fighting for a cause they deeply believe in.

The truth is that God still believes in students.

We Think of Youth Ministry as a Stepping Stone to 'Real' Ministry

Let me begin by saying, youth ministry is REAL ministry.

Although this is changing some, there remains a stigma to suggest that youth ministry is a 'less than ministry.' Yet if we took a survey of those in the Church today, many, perhaps most, would state it was during their teen years that they came to Christ. Many would also emphasize that while attending a youth ministry they were called to ministry. Finally, an overwhelming majority would affirm that a youth leader helped them walk through a difficult time in their life.

I've had the opportunity…the privilege to be involved with teens for over 30 years in some fashion. I plan to

The truth is that God still believes in students.

always be a strong advocate of youth ministry for the above reasons and others.

To the youth leader who may be struggling with thoughts that your life and/or ministry aren't making a difference, let me be the first to encourage you to not give up. There are teens that are desperately searching for someone who is willing to walk into his or her life.

Your ministry to teens is greatly needed, whether you're a volunteer, part-time, or full-time leader. If there was ever a time when teens needed to know that someone believed in them and had their back, it's now.

Social Media

As you're fully aware, just about every teen owns a smart phone nowadays. I'm forever seeing teens texting, talking, and checking their social network site as they venture through life. Phones have quickly become a necessary accessory to living out our daily lives. Don't get me wrong, I love my phone. It allows me to do the basic things a phone allows, you know…use apps, check email, text, take and post pictures, get directions, find a restaurant, pay for my coffee, make a video call, check the weather…oh, and make calls.

No, I'm not speaking against social media. I use all the current social media sites and believe there's great value in them. Here are a few reasons I mention social media as a potential hazard to discipling teens.

Today's students have access to all sorts of information at the touch of a button. Students can find a quote or statement for or against anything you say as a youth leader. As a matter of fact, they don't even have to search for it, it will find them.

Depending on the number of people they follow and who they follow, students will undoubtedly read something that sounds good but is anti – Bible, Church, Jesus.

Depending on 'who' makes the statement this only adds fuel to this potential fire of doubt and unbelief. Just try and defend Christianity against a student's favorite entertainment personality who contradicts your statement and has more followers, likes, or retweets than you.

Add to this the ease of downloading porn on your phone (the same phone that contains your Bible app) and now you're battling thoughts and pictures etched in a teen's mind as they attempt to study Scripture.

Social media is not real life. We are bombarded with everyone's highlight reel, while we are battling through unending rolls of unedited film.

As a result teens today are experiencing a greater amount of discouragement and depression. When you have a teen who posts, what they believe is a great picture, and only receives a few 'likes', they feel as if their best isn't good enough.

Here are a few hacks to help students navigate social media:

Have teens develop a habit of reading the verse of the day prior to doing anything else on their phone. There are many good Bible apps available.

Put together a social media page for teens to go to for discussion, share prayer requests and points of celebration.

Give students a few accountability sites to use and offer to receive weekly reports on their site visits.

Send a group text out once a week sharing upcoming news.

Hold various contests on who can post the best pictures, tweets, etc…from a youth event.

Encourage students to use certain #hashtags, from which you can build culture.

Challenge students to text their parents/guardians once a week to thank them for something.

Send a weekly video to encourage and challenge leaders and students.

Have a no cell phone zone. No phones can be out 15 minutes prior to or following service. This opens the door for personal conversations to take place.

There are undoubtedly other reasons discipling a teen can be a challenge but this list gives us a good idea of what we must overcome as youth leaders to reach and train up the next generation.

We must be leaders who are more committed to making life-long disciples than we are to how many students we can get to come to an event.

OVERCOMING THE CHALLENGES

Acts 17.26-27 "From one man he made all the nations, that they should inhabit the whole earth; and he marked out their appointed times in history and the boundaries of their lands, <u>that they should seek God, and perhaps feel their way toward him and find him</u>. Yet he is actually not far from each one of us…" (NIV. Emphasis mine)

God chose the times people were to be born and the places we should live! So what does this have to do with discipleship?

It is out of his great mercy that he did this. He chose the times and places that would give the best opportunity for people to seek him. Every student in your youth ministry and on the campuses in your community is positioned in this moment in history with the greatest opportunity to find God.

Understanding this truth of Scripture should serve much more than simply giving you and I confidence to do ministry. Grasping the gravity of this helps us realize that God is at work in the lives of every student in your community at this very moment, no matter what the potential obstacle! To top it off, He also chose you to reach students and make them into disciples. To quote a line from one of my favorite movies, Remember The Titans, "This is our time."

But let's take this one step further. God not only determined the places and times for individuals, but YOU are here at this exact moment in time to be an indispensable part of this harvest!

God chose you.
God appointed you to bear fruit that lasts.
God gives you what you need to make disciples.
God sets the times and places for people to live…

…so people can find Christ!

CULTURE SHAPING QUESTIONS:

What are some other challenges you face as a youth leader when it comes to discipling students?

From the list above and the list you've created what are one or two challenges you are willing to confront at this moment?

What will your plan be to overcome these challenges?

How does knowing God chose you give you confidence to lead?

SIX

CANAL SURFING

Changing culture changes destiny. Culture is a powerful tool and carries with it the ability to radically alter the future. To change to the desired future, you must transform the current culture.

Once you've decided to create culture you will need to build the platform to support and sustain it.

Over the years individuals have created some fascinating inventions. The ability to fly a ship into space and back, landing it much like an airplane, and then using it again, is one such discovery (pun intended). And although the shuttle is now retired from service, we were able to master space travel in this lifetime. What's next? Mars?

The Internet is another mesmerizing invention. The ability to gather millions of bits of information on any subject, in less than a second, continues to boggle my mind. The Internet has profoundly changed our way of life. Students can refute most anything you say by quoting the Internet. Don't believe me? Just ask your students to research how the world was created.

There they will find every conceivable solution to your statements and questions and now you are met with defending what **you** believe the Bible says. It can quickly escalate into a, 'youth leader, the Internet said' discussion.

How do you combat the Internet? Utilize the principles of social media. What principles? Actually the Bible has used these principles long before social media came about.

Think about it. Students are on social media throughout the day telling stories through pictures, videos, and posts. They are sharing their stories with the world. Students are more open, than just a few years ago, when it comes to sharing their lives. I believe social media has influenced this.

Create a Culture of Story-Telling

Allow time for students to share their stories with you and the group. Ask questions about their life. Read about them from cover to cover. A student sharing why and how they came to Christ or how Jesus healed their brother or why they are going into ministry, speaks louder than any search engine.

Tell stories from Scripture. Talk about the lives of followers in the Bible. This is one of the reasons I developed the student devotional, "PowerWalk." It contains 192 stories, told in chronological order, for students to read and reflect on throughout the year.

Unlike the future of space travel and the Internet, the spectacular structure known as the Panama Canal is also very fascinating. We take for granted cutting through a mountainous landmass of some 50 miles so ships could travel from one ocean to the other in record time. Opening the Canal saved almost 8000 miles of unnecessary travel for ships traveling from New York to San Francisco.[1]

So just what do the space shuttle, Internet, Panama Canal and discipleship have in common? Good question. I appreciate you asking. All four started as nothing more than a dream and then required a design in order to see it dedicated.

The dreaming stage brought about the initial change in the culture. The design stage put traction to the change and the dedication stage brought movement and change.

It was 1914 when the Panama Canal was forged to make a way possible for ships to navigate from one ocean to the other in the quickest possible time. It was the outcome of 34 years of work, all starting from a dream.

Don't make the mistake that many people make regarding vision and structure. The initial vision was *NOT* building the Panama Canal.

[1] http://traveltips.usatoday.com/panama-canal-61272.html

The dream was that of providing timesaving access for ships to make the trek from the Atlantic Ocean to the Pacific Ocean and back again as efficiently as possible.

Drastically reducing travel time for ships was the vision, not building a canal. As we will see later, the canal was the design-structure-platform, to put feet to the dream.

Unnecessary miles, cost and work was eliminated to take a ship to the same destination. What if those of us in youth ministry were to transfer this same ambition, creativity, and passion into discipling teens?

What if we could eliminate needless journeying and still produce bold disciples for Christ? Is it possible to make disciples who make disciples while they are still in our youth ministry?

Can we as youth leaders see MORE fruit from our students prior to graduation? Can we then send to the Church highly equipped servant-leaders? The simple answer is yes. But first we need to change the culture.

Someone has to have a dream in order to undertake a project; yet in reality, dreaming accomplishes nothing. Dreams by themselves are nothing more than a good idea. What is truly needed is the carrying out of that dream and in order to do this you must have a capable design to handle the dream.

Some time ago I heard someone suggest a three-year biblical design for disciple-making.

> *CHILD* – Moses was trained in a Levite home for the first 3 years of his life, (Exodus 2)
> *YOUTH* – Daniel and the other youth were trained for 3 years, (Daniel 1:5)
> *ADULT* – Paul received 3 years of training, (Galatians 1:18)
> Jesus walked with disciples for 3 years
> Jesus cursed the fig tree for not having fruit after 3 years, (Luke 13:6-7)

Do you have a design geared toward making disciples?

Let's dream for a moment...

What if we were able to devise a capable design, using our space shuttle or Panama Canal illustration, to move students from a specific starting point in their walk with God to a place of dedication? And what if we were able to help more students properly navigate the transition from the youth port to the Church port?

To change culture you need to create more culture. Rather than the Church trying to compete or keep in step with the world when it comes to culture, we should be dictating culture.

> *What if we could eliminate needless journeying and still produce bold disciples for Christ and His cause?*

Note in Acts 2 that the culture of Jerusalem began to change around the culture of the Church. This occurred in verse 12, "Amazed and perplexed, they asked one another, "What does this mean?" The community was asking the Church what was going on!

Create a Culture of Agents

"Typically, churches have viewed adolescents as objects of mission, not as **agents of mission**.*" -Kenda Dean*

Imagine for a moment a youth ministry made up of students passionate about becoming disciples: a group of teens who have developed as disciples and then matured in ministry assignments, leading to a healthy youth ministry culture.

I fear that too many youth structures are set up with the idea of seven years of learning (grades 6-12), and then hand them off to the big church, hoping they become servant-leaders, or simply remain a Christian.

Could we dare to dream for a period of intense learning (forging a path through what was previously thought impossible), followed by a period of growing in love, followed by fervent servant-leadership?

Is this possible to raise teens **within** our youth ministries as agents of mission and thus agents of significant culture-altering on our campuses, in our communities, and around the world?

Is it possible that once a teen graduates from our youth ministry they are fully engaged in making disciples? I believe so.

Back to our Panama Canal illustration.

The Canal is made up of three locks or levels on both the Atlantic and Pacific Oceans. Each lock raises and/or lowers the ships to the next level for safe passage. Thus a ship enters level one, transitions to level two and then three, before entering Lake Gatun.

An interesting fact about the Panama Canal is that following the first three stages of raising a ship, ships travel through Lake Gatun for 21 miles. This allows for two things to occur.

First, ships can travel at greater speeds for the 21 miles without the need to navigate through locks in the canal. Second, because Lake Gatun is a fresh water lake, ships are able to 'unload' much of the weight they've accumulated during the journey.

As ships move through the oceans they amass large deposits of barnacles. These barnacles glue themselves to ships passing through, thus weighing them down. During a ship's passage through the fresh waters of Lake Gatun, these barnacles detach themselves. As a result the ship moves faster through the second half of their journey.

As students make the journey through our youth ministries they encounter a loving God who is able to remove the accumulative weight of sin. As we disciple students, addressing past sin and addictions, we better equip them to become leaders during the second half of their journey within our ministries.

Think of it this way.

During the first part of the journey, a student is raised to a level of understanding who Jesus is, what he did, and why he did it.

The second part of their journey, they experience a greater freedom from the weight of sin. This is a direct result of knowing Jesus and a desire to turn away from sinful things. We really shouldn't expect a student to turn away from a sinful lifestyle until they travel through the first set of locks.

Finally, the third part of their journey lowers them to the second set of locks, that of a servant-leader, in order that they may help others find their way to Christ.

Discipleship doesn't end at the first level; it simply takes on a different look. The culture changes from that of a teen, encountering Jesus from a learner's vantage point, to that of a teen who now acts from a servant-leader perspective.

All this takes place in an equipping and empowering culture. Students and leaders now have a greater expectation within the youth ministry, thus more ministry is accomplished. Culture is changing!

As we will see this is the model Jesus used with his disciples. Think for just a moment about the early disciples. Did they follow Jesus because they loved him? Perhaps they fell more in love with him over time, but initially, I believe they followed because he called them to follow.

As the early disciples learned of Jesus' compassion and mission, they fell more in love with him. And generally, as they grew in love with Jesus, they grew more in love with people (sometimes that is). Recall that the Sons of Thunder, James and John, wanted to destroy a town with fire for not receiving Jesus. Sometimes loving people can be difficult.

Attempting to get students to love Jesus and others, prior to loving and learning about him, creates shallow followers. Attempting to get students to lead before they love creates harsh leaders.

Using the Panama Canal as a visual for this process we see three stages of learning, an intentional stage of freedom from past sin resulting in the student growing in love (Gatun Lake), and finally three stages of serving.

As we teach 'who' Jesus was and 'what' Jesus did, we create a culture where response is required. In other words, we have to respond to who this Jesus is and what he did for us. It's here we are challenged to fall in love with him in deeper ways.

So what does this created culture look like in a youth ministry?

> Students are called by name.
> Students respond to being called.
> Students learn who Jesus was and what his mission was.
> Students learn in a culture of love for God and people.
> Students grow deeper in their love for God and people.
> Students are set free from the weight of sin.
> Students want to serve out of love and freedom.

Many discipleship efforts gear the student to go through a series of steps to **earn** a discipleship badge. Note here that as we create culture, we simply **position** our students in such a way as to allow the Holy Spirit to work in and through their lives.

Remember the goal in building the Panama Canal was not building a great looking structure. At times youth leaders get caught up in the look of their 'structure' more than in the making of disciples. The goal was to move ships from one ocean to the next in a more efficient manner…getting ships to the next ocean faster.

The aim of youth ministry is not to have a great looking youth ministry. Discipling students can be a messy ordeal. Our aim is to move students along as learners, who know how to love, equipping them to lead as life-long followers, prior to graduating from our youth ministries.

So, back to the Internet and Space Shuttle illustrations. Like the Internet, be accessible to students. Create a culture where students know it's safe to ask you any question regarding their faith. If we don't answer their questions, who will? The Internet? You may not be as quick as the Internet, but assure them that you will take their questions seriously and act on helping them discover truth.

Create a Culture of Sanctuary

Do students know they can discuss some of life's tough issues and their questions regarding their faith in Christ?

When it comes to the Space Shuttle, create a culture of giving back to the place that sent you.

Over the years my wife and I have been able to return to the youth ministry that discipled us. We have given financially, served and helped lead mission trips with students and leaders.

Encouraging students that your youth ministry is a place to support long after they graduate helps ensure great success for generations to come. This only goes to prove that you are building the Kingdom of God and not your own.

Let's not forget that the youth ministry you currently serve in will continue long after you've moved on.

CULTURE SHAPING QUESTIONS:

Do you have a structure for discipleship in your youth ministry? What does it look like? What are the strengths? Weaknesses?

What activities, events, programs, etc do you have to help students learn who Jesus was and his mission?

How is your youth ministry creating a culture for students to express their love for God and people?

What proactive steps, programs, and activities are in place to help students be set free from sin?

List the ways you offer students opportunities for servant-leadership?

How are you communicating that students can safely ask any question and get a genuine response?

How are you challenging students to give back to the youth ministry that helped raise them as disciples?

SEVEN

YOUTH MINISTRY AND LUCKY CHARMS

Our call is to be a prophetic voice to the next generation. I don't believe we are called to deliver nice messages to students. I don't believe we are called to be event coordinators. I don't believe we are called to mold our youth ministry around what's relevant in that moment. I believe we are called to change the culture of the world around us. For us, this begins in the youth group. But it doesn't stop there.

I've run across some leaders who believe that once a student goes through a book or class, that a student suddenly becomes a disciple. This, however, only leads to sterile followers. We must build students into lifelong followers who continue to reproduce. (Um…spiritually, that is.)

As this begins to happen, your youth ministry becomes a healthier place. Your youth group *culture* begins to change.

Once the culture of your youth ministry begins to change, you will see the culture in your church and on the campus and in the community change as well.

> *Our call is to be a prophetic voice to the next generation.*

Read through the gospels and you'll find that Jesus had times when he would lecture the disciples (curriculum) and times when he would teach them in the lab (where they would experience what they just learned). Take a look at Matthew 10 and 11 as an example. Jesus lectured them on the topic of evangelism and then sent them to the lab to experience evangelism.

Matthew 11.1 "After Jesus had finished **instructing** his twelve disciples, he went on from there to teach and preach in the towns of Galilee." (NIV. Emphasis mine.)

In Matthew 11, Jesus finishes the lecture and sends them. His design was to spend time with them and then let them experience what he taught. He has always been about producing, reproducing-disciples.

Matthew 14.13-21 is another great lab example. Jesus uses this lab to teach the disciples about his provision and his ability to bring increase. Followers of Jesus need to trust God's ability to provide in the last days.

Many readers assume the passage is a lesson for the 5,000 recipients. It was not for those receiving the loaves and fish. Many of the 5,000 probably had no idea there was not enough food. This was a lab for the disciples. They knew how little food they had in their possession and then saw God multiply it.

Last day followers of Jesus need to be able to trust God at a whole different level. They need to see that God is able to make much out of a little.

Students desperately need a voice to speak into their lives and God has called you to be that voice to this generation!

Ever enjoyed a large bowl of Lucky Charms? If you've been in youth ministry for any length of time, then the answer is a resounding "yes." If you're like me, you undoubtedly tolerated the cereal part as you hunted down and devoured the marshmallowy charms.

And just like the unique marshmallows found in each box, each student in your ministry is unique in his/her design.

Each youth ministry has students who are just beginning their journey, while others are at a place where they want to be challenged as leaders. Along with these two groups you have the majority of students who fall someplace in-between.

It becomes imperative, therefore, that we design lecture and lab for each individual/group, with the idea that we constantly challenge them and look for opportunities to invite them to the next level of growth.

Create a Culture of Growth Opportunities

While youth pastoring in Princeton, New Jersey, we would meet at the church on Friday nights in order to get our students 'on the field' to stretch their faith. Our church was located directly across the street from Princeton University, in the middle of the busiest part of town and a hub of activity for teens on a Friday night. Intelligent and wealthy students surrounded our church. This combination brought about a tremendous challenge for our students when it came to defending their faith.

We divided our group into three teams. One team would stay back at the church to pray for the night, one team would serve by preparing the games, food and evening's activities and one team would go to the streets. This last team would engage in one-on-one sharing of their faith with teens on the streets. They would then invite those teens to the church for a night of food, activities, and the gospel.

During the night we would then have two or three students share their faith with the group. Students were involved in every aspect of the evening. Our leaders served only as coaches to serve and assist the students if needed.

The culture of our group began to change as a result of this. Where once our teens viewed youth group as a time to get out of the house, see who liked who, and/or play games, now we had teens who were in the game, 'on the field'. They realized that the plays we taught them over and over again on Wednesday were going to be implemented on Friday.

Repetition is a breeding ground for confidence.

Don't get hung up on the specific approach we took, it may not work in your particular zip code. Rather, engage your students on the principles of winning, building and sending. Our youth ministry should not be judged by how many seats you fill, but rather by how many students you send.

We had some students stay and pray. Some helped set up the tables, chairs and games. Others went out to share their faith and invite other teens. Who did what largely depended on where they were in their faith journey. It's to your advantage as a shepherd to know where students are in their faith development and challenge them accordingly.

There are several ingredients that determine where your students are in their faith. Understanding these is vital because it will determine how you approach discipleship. Let's examine a few ingredients necessary to understanding your approach.

Doctrine

"The theology of the youth worker is ultimately more important than his or her strategy or methodology—for it will affect everything the youth worker does." -Richard Dunn

It seems youth leaders avoid anything related to doctrine. Some cry relevance is more important than doctrine. The problem is that what's relevant today will not be two years from now. What continues to be relevant is your doctrine. Jesus' message is still as relevant today as it was 2,000 years ago.

If you believe that your prayers make a difference, you will teach (lecture) on prayer and give multiple opportunities (lab) for students to engage in prayer.

If you don't believe God heals, you will avoid this topic entirely or may even speak against it.

Thus, it's crucial that we understand our doctrine so we are better positioned to speak into the lives of the next generation. We must recognize that our doctrine is the guiding force to the discipleship culture we create.

Gifts

It's also extremely important that you recognize and utilize your spiritual gifts as you disciple others. God has given you these gifts in order to reach a world with the gospel. It only makes sense that God would use you and your gifts to make disciples.

Create a Culture of Gift Exchanges

Just as Paul encouraged Timothy to fan into flame the gift of God, we are to challenge our students to fan their gifts into flame.

2 Timothy 1.6 "For this reason I remind you to fan into flame the gift of God, which is in you through the laying on of my hands." (NIV)

God uses our gifts to bring out the gifts in others. As you discover the gifts of your students, place them in ministry positions to express those gifts.

Here are a few suggestions:

Provide opportunities for those with the gift of servant-hood to serve by setting up, tearing down, cleaning up, etc...

Give opportunities for those with the gift of evangelism to challenge the group to reach their campus.

Have those with the gift of giving to pray for and receive the offering.

Those with leadership potential should have moments to lead an activity.

Gifts of Mercy? Call them to pray with others or call others to check on how they are doing.

The Gift of Hospitality? Welcome other students as they enter the room.

Gift of Teaching? Have them share a short message with the group. If you have several with this gift, give each one the same topic and have them each share five minutes with the group. This makes up the message for the night.

Gift of Administration? Have them keep track of sign-ups, money turned in and follow up for events.

Gift of Encouragement? They are challenged to, well…encourage.

You get the idea. Fan the gift into flame and as they grow in these areas you can equip them with greater ministry roles. Give them multiple opportunities to serve and then celebrate them when they serve in their gift area.

I'm amazed at the amount of responsibilities students are given to do in the public schools and the lack of expectation we have for them in our youth ministries. Students serve in government, in clubs, as captains on teams, give speeches, raise money, and are challenged as leaders in their schools but are seldom called upon in our youth ministries. Could it be that students are used to being served rather than serve once they step through our youth ministry doors?

Our youth ministries need a 'I'm here to serve culture rather than a serve me culture.'

Could this be a reason students graduate from our youth ministries only to occupy a seat in church? Is this one reason we have a difficult time getting the adult congregation involved?

Create a Culture of Servant-Leadership

I met a youth pastor in California who regularly applied this principle. Upon meeting a new student, one of the first questions she would ask is what they liked to do or what they were good at doing. One particular youth night a new girl entered and was asked what she enjoyed doing. The new student half-jokingly answered, "I like to play cow bell."

Believe it or not, the next week the youth leader had a cowbell for the girl to play during worship! This youth leader understood the importance of creating the right culture. Getting students involved was not just a good idea. She had created a culture where everyone understood the significance of using his or her gifts for God!

There are many free spiritual gift tests available on-line. Do a search for one that suits you and your group. Then meet with your leaders to discuss each student, their gift area(s), and how you as a leadership team can fan this gift.

One idea might be to have everyone take the test but don't let them look over the results. Announce that next week you will let everyone know what their gift is. Share a message on the spiritual gifts and pass out a nicely wrapped gift box to each student. Together have the students open their gift boxes, revealing their spiritual gifts.

Depending on the size of your group you may want to encourage each leader to meet one-on-one with a student to discuss their gifts, where and how they fit in the youth ministry and a first step for activating them.

Personality

Let's face it: People come in all sorts of different and unique packages. Teens in the north are different from those in the south. West coast teens love fish tacos and east coast love cheese steaks. (Personally, I love both!)

How one was brought up also factors into our personality. Was your family one that was loud or more soft-spoken? Were you always doing things together or did you rarely see one another?

And then you have the God factor. How did God wire you? Are you spontaneous, logical, irrational, organized, task-oriented, loyal, etc…you get the picture.

All of these things play into how you will approach students in the area of discipleship. And let's not forget that how these students are wired will also determine how they will receive you as someone wishing to disciple them.

If you are more of a task-oriented, outwardly passionate, warrior mentality type, you may have a more difficult time connecting with a relationship-oriented, inwardly reserved, compassionately motivated individual.

Calling and equipping more leaders in our youth ministries allows us to be able to reach more students. As more leaders come into our ministries, they bring gifts and personalities that are different from ours. This allows them to reach teens that we might not be able to reach as effectively.

You will also find some students to be visual learners, audio learners or tactile learners (learn by touch and/or doing).

You won't be able to approach each one in the same way and expect similar results. Part of the reason for this book is to give you suggestions on how to utilize each of these learning processes in order to reach all students.

It's important to recognize this and to approach each student as an individual. This does not mean that you must only disciple students who think, act and feel like you, but you must understand that you may not entirely relate to every student.

Not every student is going to like you. As one individual stated, "you're a person, not chocolate."

I love reading through Scripture to see how the disciples related to Jesus.

> Peter had a bold and outgoing personality.
> John appeared quiet and seemed to be a bit more compassionate.
> Thomas seemed to be someone who questioned things.

This demands that we build other leaders who can then disciple those students who we are unable to reach, for whatever reason. In addition, this affords us the wonderful privilege of inspiring student leaders to disciple younger teens in our youth ministry. I believe God designed it this way to ensure we would be the body of Christ with each of us having a valuable part.

CULTURE SHAPING QUESTIONS:

Write out your doctrine. What do you believe about God and what he does in the lives of people today? What doctrinal belief(s) have you not shared with students?

Put together a sermon schedule for the coming year. Make sure you incorporate each of the doctrines you believe necessary to a teen's development as a follower.

What are your spiritual gifts?

How are you using them to create culture in your youth ministry?

What are the gifts in the other leaders in your youth ministry?

What spiritual gifts are you lacking on your ministry team?

How are you celebrating students who serve with their gifts?

What is the personality of your leadership team? What types of personalities are missing?

EIGHT

LEFT OUT OF MY RIGHT MIND

So here's a question you don't get asked every day. Are you a left-brained or right-brained thinker? Don't think this has anything to do with discipleship? Whether you're right or left brained, think again.

Matthew 22.37 – "Jesus replied: 'Love the Lord your God with all your heart and with all your soul and with <u>all your mind</u>.'" (NIV. Emphasis mine.)

Take a look at the two columns below (sorry for the two columns, right-brained people).

Left Brain	Right Brain
Practical	Jumbled
Sequential	Instinctive
Sensible	Perceptive
Diagnostic	Spontaneous
Impartial	Distorted
Looks at the parts	Looks at the whole

(Do an Internet search for a left/right brain test to see if you're right or left in your thinking.)

As you can see there is quite a difference between how the two think.

Imagine a predominately left-brained youth leader attempting to disciple a dominant right-brained student. Not to say it could never happen, it just might take additional effort for both parties. A left-brained individual might attempt to get the more artsy thinker to meet him/her at the church, in some closed-in office, the same time each week. For those of us who have had to work with right-brained people, we know that this can be a bit of a challenge.

The right-brained individual may have a difficult time adapting to someone else's schedule. They may struggle to sit in a chair and read or discuss long passages. In reality, they may simply be a different thinker from us. We shouldn't dismiss a student simply because they don't think as we do.

Of course the other scenario is just as true. A right-brained thinker may want to meet at a park with their guitar and talk about the beauty of God as seen through the trees, sky, grass, etc... This too can be a challenge if this individual is attempting to disciple a left-brained student. Both may become frustrated and the relationship may come to an end sooner rather than later.

Let's look to Jesus to gain insight. As mentioned before, Jesus' approach was BOTH lecture and lab. He would sit down with the disciples and teach, quoting Old Testament passages and words of wisdom that would later become our New Testament.

Later he would send the disciples out to "experience" discipleship. The disciples were now learning with a hands-on, tactile approach to learning. Jesus not only quoted the Old Testament but he also spoke in parables or stories. We see Jesus reaching both types of learners: the rational thinking, left-brained individual and the more random, right-brained individual.

He was visual in his methodology, often painting a picture with the truths he communicated. At times he encouraged his listeners to look or imagine something in order to clarify the message. Consider the various illustrations found in the Sermon on the Mount (Matthew 5-7) as one example.

Other times, Jesus would teach from strictly an audio means. Whether he was teaching visually, audibly, or tactile, his desire was to engage his followers. Jesus taught sitting down, standing in a boat, walking through fields, atop a hillside, hovering atop the waters of the Sea of Galilee (a definite junior high attention grabber), etc...

Jesus was intent on getting the message across to every type of learner.

Create a Culture of Multiple Learning Experiences

John 17.3 – "Now this is eternal life: that they *know* you, the only true God, and Jesus Christ, whom you have sent." (NIV. Emphasis mine.)

Remember the Bible wasn't written in English. Sometimes we translate a word and we don't completely grasp its meaning. Take the word 'know' from John 17.3. This one word carries the idea of *knowing through a process of experiences.* In other words, eternal life is understanding God through experiences.

How does this translate to us today? Understand that devotion **to** Christ is far better than having devotions **about** Christ. Allowing for creative expression and meaningful dialogue is a great initial step. Think of it as spontaneous-logic, sequential-messes or orderly-chaos.

> *Jesus was intent on getting the message across to every type of learner.*

I sometimes wonder if a task-oriented, left-brained individual created how we are told to have devotions. Nothing is wrong with that, for that particular person. But what about the student who excels at relational learning from a right-brained perspective?

My daughter, Bethany, once helped me see this in an even greater way. We were watching a reality dance show on television when one of the dancers received rave remarks from the judges and was invited to next week's show. The dancer began to jump around, flailing her arms, skipping across the room, without verbalizing a single word.

Bethany began to laugh out loud.

I asked her what was so funny as I had obviously lost something in the translation. She remarked how the girl was expressing her great excitement through her rhythmic, bodily movements rather than with her voice. Her body was screaming out with excitement, while her voice remained silent. It was only after Bethany translated what the enthusiastic dancer was saying that I was able to become a dance partner and hear the effusive screams.

Going back to Genesis we see that God was first introduced to us as Creator God. Since most of the Bible speaks of him as Redeemer, we tend to focus almost exclusively on this part of his character. He is our Redeemer AND our Creator. Don't overlook this aspect of his character.

2 Corinthians 5.17 - Therefore, if anyone is in Christ, the new creation has come (Creator): The old has gone, the new is here (Redeemer)! (NIV. Emphasis mine.)

God's creation is directly tied to his redemption.

Create a Culture of Redemptive Creativity

Some students we disciple may have a much easier time expressing their devotion to Christ through art than through reading a book about devotion to God. This is just one reason I love the arts so much. Art allows us to use the creative character of God to train up a teen in the way he/she should go. It gives teens a way to express their devotion to Christ.

It's up to us to be able to discern learning styles and then help the disciple grow in their relationship based on how God wired them in their personality and thinking. I can hear some of you crying, "But what about instilling discipline for the right-brained disciple or challenging the left-brained disciple with creativity?" My response is, "let's learn to celebrate creative-discipline."

It's a both/and, not an either/or approach to disciple making.

Consider David. He may very well have been a right-brained thinker. Writer/singer of songs, made many of his instruments, danced, and a man after God's heart. Yet he was able to be organized enough to rule a kingdom.

As he played his instruments to God, and the sheep, (and lions and tigers and bears—oh! my!), he learned discipline, warfare (fighting off those tigers, bears, lions and giants) and servant-leadership, enough to make him king.

And then you have Daniel. Prayed three times a day, most likely at the same time and same place. He is definitely one of God's great leaders. It appears Daniel was more than likely a left-brained individual. His creativity may very well have come in his prayers.

Praying three times a day meant having a creative expression in his time with God.

Discipleship approaches with creative expression engaging in both logic and jumbled thought allows us to engage the uniqueness of each student.

Occasionally one of my youth pastor friends would set up the youth room for a worship experience. A large canvas with painting supplies was set in the middle of the room. Worship music would be playing in the background. Bibles were set out are various locations and paper and pen was scattered on the floor.

Students were then encouraged to worship God through various manners using the arts. They could journal, read, pray, sing, paint, etc.

Wish to convey a passage of Scripture in a more memorable manner? Divide up into small groups, giving each group the same passage of Scripture you're going to speak on that night.

Giving each group about 10 minutes, one group prepares to act out the passage, another sings a song about it, one group writes a poem, one acts out the passage in a modern day parable, one raps, one group has each member preach a portion of the passage, etc…

Of course with some planning you can give out the passage a week or two ahead of time and groups can put together a video, pictures, painting, or human video of the passage.

Get creative. Engage all learners. Help students to love God with their entire mind.

This approach combines for the truths of Scripture with the experiences we have with God. It's all about knowing Him.

One particular night I had our small group of junior high students pile in vehicles and head to a sheep farm (I had set this up with the sheep rancher ahead of time).

Upon arrival we let the students simply walk in the sheep pen, watch the sheep, smell the sheep, and attempt to pet them. Later I had the owner talk about sheep. I then shared some verses about sheep in the Bible. We concluded by singing, "The Lord is my Shepherd."

It was a great night of learning for everyone. The sight, smell, sound, touch, music, Scripture, and insights all contributed to an unforgettable night of learning.

The night was filled with the creative aspect of God (He created sheep) and the redemptive aspect of God (we are His sheep in need of a Shepherd).

Providing meaningful and creative experiences engages students and creates a culture of learning and redemptive creativity.

A great exercise for engaging students is to have them journal in such a way as to engage both right and left thinking. Suggest a journal without any lines and have them write their thoughts and draw images on the same page.

Doing so allows for simultaneous discipline and creative thought to take place.

CULTURE SHAPING QUESTIONS:

Are you more right or left brained? How is this reflected in your ministry?

How does being right/left brained play into how you approach devotion to Christ? Are you more regimented or free-flowing in your approach?

Would you describe your youth group as more right or left brained?

What are some creative ways you could engage your students as they grow as disciples?

SECTION TWO

"DISCIPLESHIFT"

NINE

BACKYARD FOOTBALL AND FRENCH HORNS

It was my sophomore year in high school when I decided to go out for the football team. I had played football before but my only organized school experience had come in elementary school and that was flag football. And, as most every young boy had, I had played many a backyard game with friends.

What I discovered was that playing high school football was quite a few levels up from flag or backyard ball. Dominating the game in a park, with amazing catches and dazzling runs, did not easily translate to the high school gridiron.

For many teenagers, moving from the 'all pass, no rush' rules of the elementary playground ball to the 'all out hit the other player or be hit' mentality of organized ball proves to be an arduous learning curve. No longer are we drawing highly sophisticated plays in the dirt or on the back of the one kid who acted as center because he couldn't catch. Now we were forced to memorize plays, positions, blocking assignments, and handle the sometimes-unfair tactics in which our opponents play the game.

As we look to disciple teens today we realize that the elementary approach to Christianity can no longer sustain a follower of Christ as it once did. Our world is rapidly changing. As servant-leaders we must engage our students in a more formal, hands-on approach to being a disciple.

We need a comprehensive playbook with plays designed for whatever the opposition throws at us. Attempting to design a play to defeat the enemy, last minute, in a huddle, will only lead to dropped balls, missed opportunities, injured players and turnovers.

Maintaining a winning culture comes through discipline and repetition. Those of us who played sports, participated in band, strove for good grades in school or exceled at a job understand this principle.

1 Timothy 4.8 "Physical training is good, but training for godliness is much better, promising benefits in this life and in the life to come." (NLT)

Have you ever considered why a teen will rise early in the morning to practice or rehearse but has a difficult time rising to spend time with his Savior?

The Scripture above tells us that physical training is of some value; so let's take a moment to consider its value. Why will a teen rise early in the morning to get sweaty, blow their French horn on a cold day and risk lip-lock or memorize lines to a play?

As with many of you who played sports, I remember swim practices during my high school years. I had to be in the pool at 6 am. As if this wasn't torture enough our season was in the dead of winter in Nebraska. Nebraska winters are tough enough without having to jump into a pool of cold water.

We practiced for one hour before completing a full day of classes only to have to dive back in the water for two and a half more hours after school. What compels a teen to make the sacrifices he or she does today?

> They were asked by a coach
> They recognized their gift/abilities
> They wanted to get better
> They wanted to bring victory to the team
> They wanted to be with friends
> They wanted to do something fun
> They wanted to earn scholarships/recognition for the future

I'm sure there are other reasons but let's consider the ones I've listed. The issue doesn't seem to be a teen's ability to sacrifice; we all remember seeing the marching band out on a field of wet grass, practicing before the sun rose.

I believe teens make the sacrifice because they see both the short and long-term benefits of their actions. Yes, they want to be the best and to win, but it goes much deeper.

They see the value behind their sacrifices. Jesus' sacrifice and death was in part due to the fact that he saw the value of enduring the cross. Jesus understood the immediate and far reaching effects of his action.

Helping teens grasp a reason for becoming a disciplined learner and committed follower is paramount. As we help them discover their purpose in life and understand the times in which they live, they become relentless in their pursuit for his cause.

This is just one reason I believe Peter quoted from the book of Joel immediately following the outpouring of the Holy Spirit in Acts 2. Consider the fact that he could have quoted most any other passage following the baptism of the Holy Spirit. It was the divine guidance of God that Joel was mentioned.

Both Acts and Joel state that, "in the last days" the Spirit would be poured out. Let me repeat myself: if the disciples of Jesus believed they were living in the last days, how much more should we! As leaders we must help teens learn how to walk in the Spirit's power and have a last days approach to our time here on earth.

I fear that most of our time and efforts in youth ministry are aimed at simply getting teens to attend a youth service or event, read their Bible and pray, and give to missions. All worthy goals but if we are not careful these standards begin to define our approach to discipleship.

This mindset is no different from the teacher who asks a student to come to class, read the lesson, take a test and join a club. The question to ask is, why?

How many times did we have to run the same play or rehearse the same musical arrangement just so we could run the play or perform the piece one time in a game or concert? Students understand this concept more than we realize.

They have no problem preparing themselves when they know that their number will be called and they will have to take the field. We are to prepare people for works of service (Ephesians 4.12).

My concern is that many teens are never challenged or given the opportunity to demonstrate what they learned in practice. We constantly preach to them or fill them full of information but seldom, if ever, put them on the field. The full cycle of discipleship demands a winning of those who are lost, building them as disciples and then sending them out to win others.

We must shift the culture. Discipleshift is all about shifting our emphasis on how and why we disciple teens.

2 Timothy 3.1-5 "You should know this, Timothy, that in the last days there will be very difficult times. For people will love only themselves and their money. They will be boastful and proud, scoffing at God, disobedient to their parents, and ungrateful. They will consider nothing sacred. They will be unloving and unforgiving; they will slander others and have no self-control. They will be cruel and hate what is good. They will betray their friends, be reckless, be puffed up with pride, and love pleasure rather than God. They will act religious, but they will reject the power that could make them godly. Stay away from people like that!" (NLT)

> *Discipleshift is all about shifting our emphasis on how and why we disciple teens.*

The early Church began its journey with intense persecution. Do you believe that the Church that will usher in the return of Christ will experience anything less than the early Church? As prophetic leaders it is vital that we alert our students of the enemy's advances.

It is very possible that we are living in a time when we and/or our children could see the return of Christ. Having said this, I'm not, nor will I make any type of predictions. Only God the Father knows the day and time of the return of his Son (Matthew 24.36).

The signs of Christ's return are all around us. Turn on the news and glance through social media posts and you'll undoubtedly encounter multiple stories indicating this. I've come to realize more than ever that as leaders we must be prepared, and we must prepare, a generation for His return.

Thus the shift in our mission for making disciples is found in the following:

> Jesus is coming again (1 Thessalonians 4.16-17).
> We are called to make disciples who make disciples (Matthew 28.19-20).
> There will be terrible times in the last days, prior to His return (2 Timothy 3.1-5).

In light of the above, it is imperative that we understand our role as leaders. God has called us to this moment in history. Consider the fact that you and I could have been born at any other time in history, but God chose you for these days. You could have been born 300 years ago or 15 minutes from now, but God, in his infinite and redemptive thinking, chose for you to have been born for such a time as this.

Your call today is no different from the call given to individuals we read about in Scripture. Each call is God-breathed and given at the right moment in time to serve his redemptive purposes.

Just as a new figure in Scripture emerged, with a unique purpose, we must see ourselves as uniquely called for a unique purpose. As such we can no longer afford to stay the course.

We are in the final leg of the race and must run it differently than the beginning and middle portion of the race. It's not necessarily how

we start but how we finish. This is especially true as we consider how we will run this race in light of last days ministry.
Scripture tells us that many will fall away in the last days.

To suggest that we approach these last days as we've approached ministry over the past 20 years is just what the enemy would love to see. The Bible tells us that in the last days our days will grow increasingly wicked.

Consider how we are to respond to the 2 Timothy text. On the left is what the Bible states the culture of the last days will look like. To the right is the culture we should create.

> Lovers of themselves...we are to love and serve others.
> Lovers of money...we are to be givers.
> Boastful, proud...we are to walk in humility.
> Abusive...we are to walk with compassion.
> Disobedient to their parents...obey our parents.
> Ungrateful...give thanks in all circumstances.
> Unholy...live holy lives.
> Without love...love unconditionally.
> Unforgiving...forgive others.
> Slanderous...walk in grace.
> Without self-control...walk in self-control.

(This would be a great sermon series, by the way.)

With each advance of the enemy we are to take a proactive stance against the forces of evil. We are called to be light in the midst of darkness.

Many of you may remember a time when few, if any, would publically defy God. Today we see this attitude pervasive in every arena.

Slowly, over time, the enemy has created a culture of blatant disregard for God, the Bible, the Church and Christianity. We can no longer afford to disciple a generation the same way we've done if for years.

To quote an old adage, "Times are a changin."

Second Timothy proclaims that not only will last days disciples live in terrible times but Paul goes on to give us specific areas individuals will wrestle with during these last days. A careful study dealing with what students will be encountering within the last days gives the youth leader a road map for equipping them.

Let's look at a few examples in the next chapter.

CULTURE SHAPING QUESTIONS:

How can we help students see value in the daily disciplines of Bible reading, prayer and worship?

What things do you see taking place around you that makes equipping disciples more difficult?

How will you address each of these?

TEN

DUCK LIPS AND OTHER PHENOMENA

Did you know you could do a search asking the following question and get an answer? "How many selfies are taken each day?" It's over a million by the way, depending on the source.

Let's face it. We live in a different world. Well, at least I do. Some of you have grown up in a selfie environment.

My wife, Kim, is a preschool teacher. She told me the other day that kids today pose for the camera so much quicker than just a few years ago. Why? They are always having their picture taken and many preschoolers are taking their own selfies!

Another huge difference in teens today is the amount of money they receive and spend each year. The average annual income for a 12-14 year old is around $2700, and around $4900, for 15-17 year olds.[1]

Returning to our previous text we find that the 2 Timothy passage plainly states that in the last days, people will be lovers of money.

Combine this love of money with a selfie mindset and you have the makings for a generation that feels a sense of entitlement. To contend with this we as leaders must ensure that we properly train up a generation to view money with a firm biblical mindset. When a student gives to the Church or missions, we are engaging them in the very mission of God, reaching the lost.

Create a Culture of Giving

As students give, missionaries are equipped to go to the places God has called them. In addition, we are teaching students to not only be givers in a world of takers, but to have faith and believe God will provide for their every need.

[1] http://www.statisticbrain.com/teenage-consumer-spending-statistics/

Let's face it. We have no guarantees regarding the world economic situation. Our national debt continues to increase and world economies are faltering at a rapid pace. We are also witnessing a first in our nation.

It's been stated that this generation of students we are ministering too will be the first generation to have less money than their parents. As a result they will turn to someone to help meet their needs. As youth leaders we must instill within them Scriptural principles of giving and that God is faithful to meet every need.

As more of the world's economies go under, it's becoming evident that we are heading down a road where money is more sought after than ever before. Students who have been challenged to believe God to supply all their needs, and give to advance the gospel, are less likely to fall into the trap of being a lover of money.

In the last days people will be without self-control (3.3). The root of the word disciple carries with it the meaning of a disciplined learner. Mentoring students through a systematic discipleship process creates a roadway for a self-disciplined follower of Christ. It is our high privilege and responsibility to raise a generation of followers who have more than a form of godliness, but truly love and lead in the power of the Spirit.

Self-control implies that I no longer need someone else to manage me. I am now able to walk with Christ and make decisions that enable me to serve God rather than make decisions that lead to destruction. As a believer with self-control I am able to walk in and with integrity.

2 Peter 3.3 "Above all, you must understand that *in the last days* scoffers will come, scoffing and following their own evil desires." (NIV, emphasis mine)

ABOVE ALL…we must take in the fact that in the last days, scoffers will come. These scoffers will follow their own evil desires. Again, as leaders we must not only be aware of what is to come in the last days, but have a plan of action to strategically oppose what Scripture says is inevitable.

Jude 17-19 "But, dear friends, remember what the apostles of our Lord Jesus Christ foretold. They said to you, "In the last times there will be *scoffers who will follow their own ungodly desires.*" These are the people who divide you, who follow mere natural instincts and do not have the Spirit." (NIV, emphasis mine)

Two additional truths of Scripture are revealed to us from the book of Jude. Not only will scoffers come in the last days, but they will bring their evil desires (see 2 Peter 3.3 & Jude 18) *to divide the body of Christ*.

2 Corinthians 11.12-15 "But I will continue doing what I have always done. This will undercut those who are looking for an opportunity to boast that their work is just like ours. These people are false apostles. They are deceitful workers who disguise themselves as apostles of Christ. But I am not surprised! Even Satan disguises himself as an angel of light. So it is no wonder that his servants also disguise themselves as servants of righteousness. In the end they will get the punishment their wicked deeds deserve." (NLT, emphasis mine)

Paul dealt with false teachers and as we move closer to the return of Christ we find ourselves equipping a generation of students who will deal with false teachers in greater measures. These false teachers have two goals: to mislead followers and divide the body of Christ.

Create a Culture of Unity.

In addition, false teachers do not have the Spirit. It goes without saying, but in these last days we must have a generation who live and walk in the Spirit!

We must engage a generation of students whose lives are marked by the fruit of the Spirit, who are sensitive to the leading of the Spirit, and walk in the Spirit.

Simply giving a set of rules for teens to follow may be a good start in the discipleship process but we must teach this generation how to walk in a spirit of discernment. Let me share a personal illustration regarding walking in discernment.

I realize some will disagree with me on this approach but I have actually sat down with my own kids to watch an R-rated movie. Some may say that no Christian should watch movies that carry more than a PG-13 rating. My problem with this approach is that as soon as you suggest that disciples not view R-rated movies, you automatically give approval for every PG and PG-13 movie.

There have been times when I've had to walk out of a theater or turn off the television on a program that was PG or PG-13. There have also been movies that carry an R-rating that I felt were of benefit for my teen to see.

One of my daughters was going through a time when she thought the world revolved around her and that she had a rough life. She was experiencing all sorts of first world pains and needed a reality check.

So I sat down with her and watched the movie, "The Patriot." I wanted her to see what others sacrificed in order that we could enjoy freedom. Following the movie we sat down to discuss it and the impact it had on our lives.

My wife and I did the same with our girls when "The Passion of the Christ" was released.

I'm not suggesting that we gather our students and show them R-rated movies to discuss. What I'm attempting to show is that teaching a student how to discern good and evil prepares teens in a much greater way.

As I mentioned earlier, I did not grow up in a Christian home so my listening and viewing habits were questionable. As I grew in my relationship with the Lord I remember how the lyrics to some of the songs I listened to as a teen suddenly seemed inappropriate. What changed was my ability to discern good and evil and make decisions that would help my walk with Jesus.

Mentoring students in their choice of movies, music, dress, speech, etc…requires we teach them how to discern the spirit behind it. It's much easier to simply make a rule as to what movies to watch, what music is acceptable, what length a pair of shorts should be, what words are questionable, etc…

The basic problem with this approach is that it only addresses the outward appearance. In essence we create a culture of, "I'm sitting down on the outside, but standing up on the inside," disciple.

Creating a culture where students learn to walk with the Spirit is critical to their growth and ability to discern.

OTHER PHENOMINA

Did you see the video about the guy who took a selfie of himself while inside a tornado? Perhaps you viewed the video of a pig rescuing a goat from drowning? Remember the sharks in the New York City subway system?

Maybe it was the Chilean coastline tsunami that caught your attention? There are videos and photos meant to look genuine but are in truth far from it. In the meantime millions of people are misled.

The brilliance of technology has made it possible to convey images previously unimaginable as being real. I believe using the power of technology to portray false and divisive stories will be a major tool of the enemy in the days ahead.

How many times have we had a student share with others something they saw on the Internet that they were convinced was true? Only later did they hear that the picture they saw or the video they watched was a hoax.

The enemy desperately desires to deceive individuals into believing things and has 'proof' through video! Helping students walk in discernment will guard them against misleading events.

> *Creating a culture where students learn to walk with the Spirit is critical to their growth and ability to discern.*

Create a Culture of Discernment.

One idea is to show your students a few videos, some of which are true and some that are false but appear to be true. Talk about how to determine if a video or picture is true or not. Discuss how to discern whether what they are seeing is true or not and what tools exist that they can use to help them.

Then apply these principles to the idea of walking in discernment.

I urge you to pray and fast as never before for the students God has placed in your care. YOU were chosen for this task, at this time. Let's not allow the enemy to gain ground during our watch, but let's clear a pathway for the Holy Spirit to move in greater ways in these last days.

One of the most prolific passages on the last days is found in the 24th chapter of Matthew.

Jesus communicates to His disciples and to us today that in the last days there will be wars, rumors of wars, famine, and earthquakes in various places. These are all signs of His coming. I think all of us would agree that our world is experiencing more of each of these signs. According to Scripture, we will continue to see more of this as well.

Understand that my purpose in bringing this to our attention is not to be an alarmist. Nor is it my attempt to breed fear in order to state my case. Rather, I am simply putting the need to make disciples in the context of the days ahead.

Jesus did this, as did Paul and other writers of the New Testament. Since the end is near, we haven't much time and must be about our Father's business...making life-long followers of Jesus, who walk with Spirit-led discernment.

Found within the signs that Jesus gave us regarding his return we see one particular sign repeated over and over again. Jesus warns us in Matthew 24, verses 4, 5, 11, 23, 24, and 26, of false teachers or prophets.

Clearly Jesus is sending the message that false teachers are not only a sign we are near the end, but that we need to watch out for these false prophets as they will divide the body with even the elect falling away.

Last days disciples will be people who love the Church, desire to serve God and the body of believers and reach people with the gospel. They will not be out to build their name but rather the name of Christ. The Church is to take on his name as the bride takes on the name of her groom.

This demands that we produce disciples who are in tip-top discipleshape. This becomes our focus in the next section.

CULTURE SHAPING QUESTIONS:

What are other indicators do you see in Scripture that we are living in the last days?

How does your view of discipling teens change when viewed in the context of last days?

What are some ways we can disciple teens to be last days followers?

How are you communicating this?

How can you begin to teach students to walk with discernment?

SECTION THREE

"DISCIPLESHAPE"

ELEVEN

SIX-PACKS AND BICEPS

I believe making disciples while teens are still in middle and high school is far more strategic than waiting until they reach the college years. We cannot afford to wait until college to equip students against the philosophy they will encounter in the college classroom. Nor can we wait until they become adults in our churches before we challenge them to get into discipleshape.

Create A Culture of Runners

I lived in Phoenix, Arizona from fourth grade through half the year of my sixth grade year. It was during this time that I was introduced to my gym teacher named Mr. Nelson. Of course, this was in the day when students had gym class and were fortunate enough to participate every day.

Mr. Nelson was your typical elementary school gym instructor. Adorned with white, canvas tennis shoes, white tube socks, with blue and gold strips at the top and pulled tightly to mid-calf, double-button softball shorts and a polo shirt…tucked in, baseball cap, clipboard, and of course, a whistle around his neck.

Every day, without exception, every student in Mr. Nelson's gym classes ran a mile prior to engaging in the remaining 35 minutes of activities. Yes, you read that right. Every day as a nine-year-old, I ran a mile, in the often 100-degree heat of Phoenix. Good thing it was a dry heat!

By the time I was 10 years old I was able to run the mile in six minutes. I attribute this to Mr. Nelson's passion for seeing to it that every student in his gym class get into shape.

This passion of Mr. Nelson's resulted in our school winning most every competition we entered. From cross-country to football, from basketball to track and field, we dominated the other Phoenix schools.

I realized just how hungry the coaching staff was for victory during my sixth grade year. It was during one of our football games that the other team scored. Not a big deal you say? What you don't understand is that our school hadn't been scored on in years. We won every game and shutout every team.

To say that our coaches were upset would be an understatement. We still won the game but spent the next week enduring longer and more intense practices. Not only did we win the remainder of our games that year, but no other team scored on us the remainder of the year.

It was during this time that I learned the value of working hard for what you believe in and believing in what you valued. I still remember sitting on the grass of Longview Elementary/Jr High, listening to the coaches tell us we had to get better and that no one would score on us again that year. It left quite an impression on me and I still remember it to this day.

What I learned as a young boy was the value and purpose of proper preparation, a winning attitude, discipline, and endurance through physical exercise. This has stuck with me my entire life. As a result I still enjoy and play sports and exercise to this day.

Preparing students for last days ministry will demand of us as youth leaders that we produce followers with the spiritual tenacity required to win a world to Christ and his cause. This too can only come through hard work, discipline, a winning attitude and a culture of commitment. I call it Discipleshape.

Without a doubt, exercise and the suitable equipment needed to get into shape has significantly changed over the years.

We've learned quite a bit and the evolution of training and equipment has shown us this. What if we could take the principles learned from gym class and apply them to helping our students get into the spiritual shape they will need to be in for these last days?

What's your definition of a top athlete? Whether you say a professional athlete, someone able to climb Mt. Everest, a formula one driver, an Olympic gold medal winner, etc... each one must have these ingredients to acquire peak performance.

> Strong Core
> Steady Balance
> Extreme Stretching
> Vibrant Cardio
> Disciplined Mind

Take one of these away and you drastically reduce the effectiveness of the athlete. So how does this translate into producing strong followers? Let's take a look.

In addition to loving God with all our heart, soul and mind, Luke 10.27 tells us we are to love the Lord with all strength.

We are pretty good at challenging students to love God with our heart. Some do a good job at engaging a student's mind as well. So what does it mean to love God with all our strength? I like one definition I came across: having a capacity for endurance.

Christianity is not a sprint. It's a race that lasts a lifetime.

So let's look at the five ingredients in the making of a student we want to get into discipleshape. They must have a...

Strong Core

I once heard of gym owner who would watch as each man entered the weight room to see which piece of equipment they would go to first. Without hesitation, if the would-be weight lifter started with curling, for that bigger bicep look, the owner would kick him out of the gym. The gym owner's rational was based on the need to build a strong, healthy core prior to building the "showy" bicep muscles.

He had a passion for seeing young men build muscle in the correct order of importance. The art and science behind core work suggests that building a strong core allows for the proper development of all other muscle groups. It also reduces the possibility of injury and the misleading comments given by others of how well built someone was, when they lacked the core to sustain proper muscle development.

Building core strength, those muscles that aren't seen to the physical eye but are much needed to meet the demands placed on a body during strenuous times, is indispensable. Getting a student into discipleshape, specifically shaping their spiritual core requires that we as youth leaders serve as trainers. Core objectives become our initial training devices.

Do students in your ministry have a firm understanding of the Bible and doctrinal truths?

Let's be honest. Most youth leaders would agree that today's student sees truth as relative, with everyone having their own definition of truth. Again, I draw your attention to the need for a strong core, namely understanding of the Bible.

In the last days there will be false prophets and teachings. Without a fixed grasp of biblical truths, students will be left tossed and blown around by every wave of new teaching (Ephesians 4.14).

You've heard it before but rules without relationship leads to rebellion. We can't raise a generation with a set of rules without engaging them in meaningful relationships. Relationships must be built with others in order to pave the way for notable conversation of who Christ is in an individual's life.

Thus a core objective is to train our students to value and continually remain connected in their relationship with God. To attempt to teach Scriptural truths outside of a relationship has the potential of appearing legalistic.

Giving understanding to our need to strengthen relationships is just the first step. Thus our worship toward God is core in our becoming his disciple. It's been said you become what you worship. Our lives and the lives of our students are transformed in and through our worship of and obedience to God. As long as we prioritize worship and obedience for our students, we continue to solidify their core.

Worship is so much more than a 20-minute sing along on a Sunday or Wednesday night. Worship is obedience to God and his Word. We celebrate in our singing to Him because of who he is and because of our desire to obey.

Loving God is relatively easy. Loving people can prove to be a much more arduous task. Or at least that's how it feels at times. Yet Jesus tells us that there is no greater commandment than to love God and love people (Mark 12.30-31). One cannot exist without the other.

Loving people will become much more difficult as we venture into these last days.

Remember from our previous texts that many scoffers will come with one of their sole purposes to divide the body. Unfortunately, many of us have already been involved in heated and sometimes divisive conversations with other members of the Church.

Teaching students how to handle relationships with parents, (Recall 2 Timothy 3.2, tells us that in the last days individuals will be disobedient to their parents), how to navigate relationships with authorities, and how to engage in relationship with those who don't yet know Christ is critically necessary.

We must create a culture where students develop discipline to run hard after God every day. The daily exercise from engaging in God's Word, building healthy relationships, and passionate worship all contribute to a healthy core and ultimately a healthy disciple.

I remember one particular day I took one of our students to lunch to spend time together. I believed he had a call of God on his life and wanted to take some time to encourage him. It was during this season in my life that I had started thanking police officers and firemen for their service to our community.

As we walked in to have lunch, I noticed two officers having lunch.

As I had done several times before, I walked over to thank them for serving our community. One of the officers was very nice and asked me several questions. The other officer seemed bothered by my unannounced interruption. He just stared at me.

After a few moments of interaction I left to sit down and enjoy lunch with my student. As we were eating and discussing God's call, the friendly officer left, leaving the one officer who had only stared at me up to this point. A moment later he got up from his table, approached us, and knelt down.

The officer asked me if I knew what they were talking about when I interrupted. I told him that I didn't and simply wanted to say thanks. He then proceeded to tell me that the other officer was sharing that Jesus was coming back and asked him if he was ready for Christ's return. Tears began to form in his eyes as he looked at me and said, "and then you walked up…and you're a minister." (The other officer had asked what I did for a living.)

I had no idea what they were discussing or where this officer was on his life journey. As the officer left I was able to talk with the student across from me about a number of things when it comes to following Jesus. The most important lesson was and is loving God and loving people.

Loving God and people is the heart of the disciple. It's core to our growth. It's WHO we are, not just WHAT we do. As we grow in love we learn discipling principles to help us develop core beliefs as followers.

Create a Culture of Identity

I trust you didn't read through that last paragraph too quick. We get it backwards when we try to get a teen to believe in something without first helping them know they are loved and then fall in love.

Too many times a youth leader will teach WHAT students are to do before teaching them WHO they are in Christ. This is developing the biceps before the core.

I came across this illustration some time ago. Note that first God spoke of identity. He then announced his love/relationship with him and then spoke of mission.

Matthew 3.17 – "And a voice from heaven said, 'This is my Son, whom I love; with him I am well pleased.'" (NIV)

Identity – "My Son"
Intimacy – "Whom I love"
Image – "Well Pleased"

More and more today, teens are wrestling with their identity.

Sometimes in our youth ministries we try and get teens to reach and love others first. The problem is they are still trying to understand their identity and how to be loved. This is a huge issue in our world today.

Students are much more likely to engage others with the gospel as we teach them who they are in Christ and that they are deeply loved by God.

I learn to love because…I learned He first loved me.

On several occasions I have asked our server if we could pray for them while we pray for our meal. As they bring us our meal, I'll simply tell them that we are going to pray for our food and want to know how we can pray for them.

One moment that stands out occurred when our server sat beside me and began to cry. She told me about her struggles as she grabbed my hand to ask for prayer. Love requires a risk. Jesus took this risk for us. As followers we risk most when we love most.

We stop making disciples when we become more concerned with how many are coming to our youth ministries rather than how many we are sending from our church into a hurting, dying world to LOVE.

We were never meant to live out our Christianity within the walls of our Church. We learn to run by being outside!

Last days Christians cannot afford to be wimpy Christians. Consider this: If you were the enemy and knew your time was short, would you not do anything and everything to stop the movement of the opposing army? Of course you would. Our enemy is throwing out every piece of artillery he can in these last days to stop the movement of God's people.

He has no reason to save any weapons or strength for later. If he cannot win, and we fully understand he doesn't, he will do everything he can to minimize the impact of his enemy, namely those who follow Christ.

At the same time we serve a God who has a sacrificial heart for people. Second Peter 3.9 tells us that God doesn't wish for anyone to perish. He is a loving God and wants to spend eternity with all people.

You can already see how this is, and will, lead to a greater spiritual warfare and worldwide conflict as we live in the last days.

Acts 2.17 "'And *in the last days* it shall be, God declares, that I will pour out my Spirit on all flesh, and your sons and your daughters shall prophesy, and your young men shall see visions, and your old men shall dream dreams.'" (ESV, emphasis mine)

In the last days, God is pouring out his Spirit. As time moves along and as we eagerly await the return of Christ, we see an increase in the work of the Spirit. Space does not permit to go through a Scriptural study of it at at this point, but the evidence is before us.

With each new day we have the opportunity to encounter the Spirit of God in immeasurable ways. This brings incredible growth in our lives and a greater desire to serve God and others.

It's crucial that we teach our students how to engage their core with and in God's Word rather than solely teaching them God's Word once a week. Yes, we must continue to teach, but let's be proactive regarding the developmental aspect of a disciple by discipling them on how to correctly use Scripture and in turn, to truly understand what they believe.

Here are a few suggestions on how to engage student's core.

Take time to teach students how to use and read their Bible. This can be done one-on-one or in a small group. It may look something like this.

First week go through books in Old and New Testament, review maps, cross references, etc. This will depend on each student's Bible. It's important they understand how to USE their Bible (There are also some great online Bible commentaries that can help). We can't always be with one of our students when a friend asks a question of them or they are in need of an answer for themselves to one of life's questions. We must equip our teens on how to use this foundational app.

During the second week have students look up verses on certain subjects or themes and then take time to discuss how these sections could be valuable if faced with questions from others regarding their faith or why they believe certain things. For example, teach them how to find a verse on salvation or faith, worship or trust, healing or love.

In the third week go through any study notes, glossary of terms, and concordance. Read through a chapter, stopping to look up cross-references and terms. This will empower students.

The next week challenge them to begin reading through a book of the Bible at a time. I like starting students with the book of Mark. It's fast paced and gets right into showing who Jesus was and what he did.

Imagine taking every new sixth grader and new student in your youth ministry through a few weeks of a basic Bible core training.

Picture sitting down with each one and the first thing they learn is HOW to use their Bible.

Another idea is to have them download a Bible app and look through the many youth devotionals available. Perhaps have your entire group go through the same devotional together with a time of celebration at the end.

Conclude these moments with a time of prayer over what you've just read or studied. Challenge them, by name, to be students of God's Word. And finally, regularly acknowledge the growth you see in them.

Steady Balance

Knowledge of the Bible without application leads to legalism. Embracing experiences without a solid Scriptural understanding leads to wavering faith. We must have steady balance.

The challenge for us as youth leaders is to provide this balance in our youth ministries. We've identified the need for core Scriptural truths in our lives, but we must couple these with experiences.

Engaging worship opportunities, camps, conventions, life-giving activities, periodic events, and meaningful retreats and outreaches give us healthy experiences and lead to a well-balanced teen.

Every now and then I'll hear a youth leader say they don't like camps or conventions because they are all experiential and full of hype and excitement. We not only need experiences, we were created for them. Jesus often approached teaching a truth by first having followers experience that truth.

Having said this let me ask a question. Have you ever been to a baseball game or other sporting event? Did you cheer? Did you get out of your seat and yell for your team? Did you buy a hot dog, nachos and soda? OK, maybe the last question doesn't apply, but you see where I'm heading.

My point is that just as in life, we all need experiences that support our beliefs. Celebratory experiences reinforce our beliefs. What good is it if we believe a team is the best team on paper, but never show our support or experience the game itself?

We must allow students to fully engage in experiences that demonstrate what they believe to be true.

Take a look at Acts 2 and you'll find this balance in action. The early Christians found a way to have Scriptural truths and faith-filled experiences compliment each other as they walked out their salvation.

> *Knowledge of the Bible without application leads to legalism. Embracing experiences without a solid Scriptural understanding leads to wavering faith. We must have steady balance.*

The Acts 2 Church saw the importance of this. Take a look at Acts 2.42-47, "They (the early Church) devoted themselves to the apostles' teaching (core) and to the fellowship (experiences), to the breaking of bread (experiences) and to prayer (experiences)." This was a proactive step on their part. They experienced the selling of goods (experiences), (v 45), they met together (experiences) with glad and sincere hearts (v46), and praised God (experiences) and enjoyed (experiences) the favor of people (v 47). (Additional notes mine)

There was a healthy balance of core teaching and experiences as they shared life together.

In the next chapter we will look at the other qualities necessary to building a healthy disciple.

CULTURE SHAPING EXPERIENCES:

Consider incorporating the following activities and experiences in your youth ministry.

Cross-cultural mission experiences

Giving to missions and compassion based ministries

Campus and community outreaches

Prayer and worship experiences

Retreats, conventions and camps

Social justice causes

Neighborhood service projects

Food or social media fasts

What are some additional experiences you can create for your youth ministry?

TWELVE

GROWING DISCIPLE = HEALTHY CULTURE

Extreme Stretching

Without flexibility, muscles never reach their full potential. Flexibility does not mean watering down anything. As a matter of fact, it means growing stronger in my core convictions and understanding the difference between convictions and preferences.

It is of tremendous benefit to challenge (stretch) students in their faith.

Create a Culture of Faith

Occasionally I would do a little exercise called four corners. One corner was labeled strongly agree, one was agree, one was named strongly disagree and the last was disagree.

Students would stand in the middle of the room while I read a statement. A statement might be, "It is acceptable for Christians to drink alcohol as long as they don't get drunk."

Students then had to go to one of the corners and be ready to defend their position. As you can imagine this would lead to some interesting discussions. Doing so gave me an idea of where the group stood on issues and what I needed to address while providing students a chance to hear from other students. This exercise stretched us as a group, forcing each student to think through their beliefs and convictions.

After five minutes of discussion or so I offered a chance for students to change their minds and move to another corner of the room. Each time anywhere from a few to several students would move to another corner. This gave me an opportunity to ask why they moved. What was said that brought them to a point to change their thinking?

Providing students opportunities to stretch their spiritual muscles serves to strengthen their faith.

I have a specific belief concerning my stance on the Baptism in the Holy Spirit, but it will never bring division between me and another member of the body of Christ. Remember, in the last days the enemy will work overtime to divide the body. My preference is to sing certain songs in worship or to connect students to God in a particular way in the altars.

Don't confuse convictions with preferences. Neither will I allow preferences to divide.

I must remain flexible on certain issues, always preferring the weaker brother (Romans 14, 1 Corinthians 8).

Some may ask, "What about standing for what you believe?" Great question. This comes through developing our core. What are core beliefs? These are the truths we disciple into students in order that they stand firm in their faith.

Students must be challenged to continually build their core AND continually be stretched. After all, we want our students to be able to lift heavier weights. Perhaps you have held the belief that God no longer heals people and have taught this to your students. Chances are they will believe this because you taught it. Then one day you read in Scripture a verse that convicts you that healing is for today. This causes you to re-examine your stance on healing.

You held a core belief AND you continued to stretch your faith by allowing God to speak into your life regarding his Word. Without a doubt there are core truths that we will always adhere too. Salvation through Christ alone is one such example.

We have a tendency to believe the first 'truth' we hear as truth. We must continually challenge our faith and the faith of our students to be stretched. Truth doesn't change but our understanding of it may.

Just as the four corners exercise showed us, we all have beliefs, we must be ready to defend those beliefs, and we must be open to allowing others in the body of Christ to share their beliefs with us.

We may not change our minds on an issue but by discussing our beliefs we avoid bringing division in the body of Christ. Never be afraid to change your stance on something you held to be true in the past just because it was the first way you heard it expressed.

As you can see, challenging students to stretch can actually strengthen their spiritual muscles and they become stronger.

As mentioned before, balance in my walk comes by growing in my Scriptural understanding and my experiencing the Holy Spirit in times of worship, preaching, and response to his Word. On the other hand, flexibility in my walk comes by stretching my faith, allowing more of the Spirit in my life and yielding myself to the Spirit.

Just as physical stretching is uncomfortable at times, so is stretching ourselves spiritually. Yet the more we stretch ourselves the further we can reach!

Here are some other exercises to get students to stretch their faith.

Encourage students to read the Bible and bring a question about what they read to discuss. This encourages students not only to read the Bible but to seek out questions aimed at stretching them.

Have students ask others in their school if they believe the Bible is true today and if not, why not? Have them bring these thoughts to group to discuss in order to give a response.

While meeting with a student or a few students ask them the one thing they have the hardest time believing about Christianity or the Bible. Talk about it with them.

Pray big prayers. Challenge students to stretch their faith and believe for miracles. Keep a prayer journal or prayer wall in your youth room and record the date when prayers are answered.

Have students attend a Christian event on their campus. This could include See You at The Pole, a campus club for Christians, Fellowship of Christian Athletes, etc…Talk about their experiences and what, if anything, stretched their thinking regarding their faith.

Encourage students to write a research paper or personal faith story for a class assignment.

Discuss current events in our world and talk about them in light of good and evil, God's purposes, what the Bible says, and how the enemy deceives others.

Never be afraid to discuss the issues that students are battling in their faith journey. If you don't know how to address a particular topic tell them you'll get back with them. Do some research or talk with a seasoned individual for help.

Vibrant Cardio

Cardio exercises help strengthen and enlarge the heart muscle. This should be one of our greatest goals as disciple makers, to strengthen and enlarge the hearts of followers.

To be a top performing athlete one needs increased cardio production. To continue to grow spiritually, one needs to engage their heart. Heart exercises come through a variety of ways in the physical.

Running, plyometrics, aerobics, stair and mountain climbing, cycling and swimming all help improve cardio function. In much the same way there are spiritual exercises that help to strengthen the heart of students.

Create a Culture of Compassion

Enlarging the hearts of our students creates a breeding ground for unity and fulfilling the mission of Christ. These are two of the most important ingredients in the life of a healthy disciple.

Consider this.

With an increase cardio capability disciples are able to sustain their walk with greater enthusiasm. For those who are runners there are few things more enjoyable than recording your best time in a 5K.

This comes only through increasing your practice regiment, distance, and speed. Of course as you do this you challenge your heart to keep pace with your body and your desire to run faster.

As we challenge students to run faster and further, we are training them for a Christianity that is more a marathon than a sprint. We need to train students for the long haul. One way we do this is to teach them to engage their hearts throughout the day rather than a few select times during the week. Allow me to give a few examples.

Many a youth ministry will take their students through an outreach to a specific group of people. This may include a children's outreach, foreign mission trip to a third world country, or an outreach to homeless. All worthy causes and each one brings great benefits for students and leaders alike.

The potential danger in this cardio approach is that is teaches students that outreach is an event rather than a lifestyle. This approach to sharing the gospel would be equivalent to the person not running for several weeks and then entering a race for which they didn't train.

We are to be salt and light each day. Teaching our students to reflect Christ in every situation and with each individual requires a strong heart.

> *Enlarging the hearts of our students creates a breeding ground for unity and fulfilling the mission of Christ.*

We better equip and prepare our students as followers as we engage students in heart pumping, lifestyle evangelism.

Here are a few activities to increase the cardio activity of your students.

Have students set an alarm on their phone each day that reminds them to pray a simple prayer. In this prayer students ask God to open doors for them to share their faith story with others. Doing this helps students proactively look for opportunities throughout the day.

Encourage students to give thanks for their lunch at school. Doesn't have to be a loud prayer but a simple prayer of thanksgiving. This opens doors for conversations with other students.

If students are part of a sports team or school activity, have them lead the team or group in prayer prior to the start.

Students can text a friend each day letting them know they prayed for them.

Mow, shovel snow, rake leaves, clean gutters, wash windows for a neighbor.

Give a birthday card to teachers. Write an encouraging message on the inside.

Arrive five minutes early to work and stay five minutes later.

Give clothes and food to a local compassion ministry.

Take a friend to coffee and share their faith with them.

Pray for another country or people group each day.

Challenge students to give their largest offering to a mission project.

These are just a few ideas to encourage students to make a daily connection with God, while demonstrating their faith. In other words, they're being salt and light. Each activity is geared to engaging their heart on a daily basis.

Over time their faith is strengthened and they will find themselves connecting and engaging in stronger ways. Of course continue with the mission trips, compassion ministry, outreaches and periodic activities. These activities combined with smaller, daily exercises develop a well-rounded disciple. The everyday cardio experiences help build a stronger heart for the bigger races in life.

Disciplined Mind

Perhaps the toughest discipline to engage your students in is a disciplined mind. Students can show up to youth group saying and doing all the right things while having an undisciplined mind. Our role as leaders is to help them think healthy thoughts.

A simple definition of integrity is, "the state of being whole." A lack of integrity develops when our feelings and thinking don't match.

Integrity is the discipline of matching our heart-feelings with our brain-thoughts.

My thinking and my feelings are to line up to match my walk with Christ. This means my logical choices and my emotional decisions are to reflect my walk with Christ. As we go about making disciples who have self-control we empower them to love the Lord with all their heart, soul and mind (Matthew 22.37). Everything working in harmony.

Proverbs 4.23 – "Above all else, guard your heart, for everything you do flows from it." (NIV)

You may believe this verse better fits in the heart cardio section but I believe it is a better fit here. The verse mentions we are to guard our hearts. Guarding our hearts involves having the right mindset. We guard our hearts by thinking right thoughts and having right attitudes.

So what are some exercises we can give to teens to help them develop a disciplined mind?

Connect with God's Word each day, even if just for five minutes. I'd rather see a student read five minutes a day than read once a week for 35 minutes.

Pray God's Word. Choose a verse or two to pray into their lives. Using Proverbs 4.23 might look something like this.

"God, today I ask that you help me guard my heart by keeping my thoughts and speech pure. I realize that everything in life flows from my heart so I ask that you help me with this."

Perhaps once a month choose a verse for the entire youth group to pray into their lives. Lead them in this and do it as a group. Then challenge your students to do this on their own a few times a week.

Practical steps to guarding your heart are found in the next few of verses from Proverbs 4.

"Keep your <u>mouth</u> free of perversity; keep corrupt talk far from your lips. Let your <u>eyes</u> look straight ahead; fix your gaze directly before you. Give careful <u>thought</u> to the paths for your <u>feet</u> and be steadfast in all your ways. Do not turn to the right or the left; keep your <u>foot</u> from evil." (NIV. Emphasis mine)

This little exercise helps focus a teen's mind around searching God's Word for the 'how to's.'

Encourage students to play worship music each morning, as they get ready for school or work.

Challenge students to listen to a chapter of the Bible as they ride to school or work.

Teach students to journal. Journaling engages both right and left brained thinking.

Memorize God's Word.

Meditate on a passage of Scripture dealing with our thinking each day for a week or month. Take a passage like 1 Corinthians 13.4-8 or Philippians 4.8-9 and meditate on it.

While a youth pastor in New Jersey I challenged my students to memorize Psalm 139 in a week. Anyone who memorized more than me received a gift. Although no one student had the entire chapter memorized, several tried and had at least a few verses memorized. It proved to be a creative way to engage everyone in our group to start a journey of memorizing Scripture.

Give students safeguards. With all the technology available to students these days, many struggle to keep their minds guarded. There are several accountability websites and apps that can help students learn discipline. Knowing that you have access to the sites they visit helps them guard what they view.

Fast social media one day a week, one week a month, one month a year, etc…

Teach students to listen to the words and messages in the music they listen to and the movies they watch. Perhaps have them write out the lyrics to a song they like. Seeing the words is different from listening to them. Teaching discernment goes further than telling them what shows they can watch or what music they can listen too.

Give students prayer triggers. When a teen thinks an inappropriate or damaging thought about themselves or someone else, have them use it as a trigger to pray for someone or quote a verse of Scripture. Bad thoughts trigger a prayer!

Encourage students to practice gratitude.

CULTURE SHAPING QUESTIONS:

How are students engaging in extreme stretching?

How are you challenging your students with vibrant cardio?

What are ways you helping students develop disciplined minds?

THIRTEEN

INSERT SMILING EMOJI

As your teens become healthier in their walk with Jesus, they become stronger followers and are able to run harder and for longer distances. Just as there are certain theological truths you want your teens to grasp, there are certain non-negotiable disciplines you'll want to see develop within the hearts and minds of your students.

Beside each of the four disciplines draw an emoji image that best reflects how well they are present in the culture of your youth ministry.

Connect

It's vital that our students learn to connect with God on a regular basis. Given that students come with widely unique personalities and gifting, we must help students embrace connecting that is both Scriptural and fits within their prayer-communication style.

Just as one child comes to their father in one way and another child from the same home approaches dad in a different way, we all speak with our heavenly Father uniquely. It's important that we understand we are not discipling a student to be like us or do everything like us but rather we are attempting to develop them as disciples. In this case, we are aiding them in the discipline of prayer.

I'm pretty sure the way Peter prayed was different from the way John, James, Abraham, Daniel, Esther or Paul prayed.

Some may find a walk in the park is the best way to communicate. Others may enjoy kneeling by their bed or sitting quietly. Some will pray with a loud voice and others may speak with God more conversationally.

Whether we pray loudly or softly, in the church or at home, we are all to approach with confidence.

Hebrews 4.16 – "Let us then approach God's throne of grace with confidence, so that we may receive mercy and find grace to help us in our time of need." (NIV)

So as someone wishing to disciple, why not take a prayer journey with those you are discipling? For example, your group prays every day, but each day has a unique approach to where and how you pray. One day take a walk, the next kneeling beside your bed, the next sitting outside, etc....

Create a Culture of Praying Outside the Lines

At times I would take students to church with me to pray in the sanctuary, challenging them to pray an hour. Other times I would go to their homes and pray with them in their living room. I would also pray with students for their campus as I drove them to their school in the mornings. During some of our retreats we would send the teens off for an hour on a 'vow of silence.' These times were set aside to simply listen. Students would journal what they believed God was speaking.

Here are some ideas:

Have students set their alarm to go off five minutes prior to getting up each morning. Encourage them to connect with God before doing anything else that day.

Encourage students to journal. Journaling doesn't have to be on a lined page either. Some students will engage more frequently by having freedom to write and/or draw their thoughts and prayers outside the lines.

Make it a point to pray with every student in your youth ministry outside of the church. Praying with a student at a coffee shop is different from praying with them at church. Doing so allows your teens to experience prayer in a variety of situations.

It also allows you as the leader to have a better idea as to where each student is concerning his or her prayer life. You are helping students connect with God in prayer.

Encourage students to play worship music as they get ready for school each day.

Challenge students to pray the lyrics they hear in the worship songs they hear.

Direct students to a Bible app. Prior to looking at any social media that day, have them read through the verse of the day several times.

Set up a text reminder to send to each student every morning. It simply encourages them to make a connection that day.

Capture

Help students to capture God's Word for their life. Challenging students to read and apply God's Word is necessary for growth. Recall our definition of disciple.

"A disciple is one who embraces and assists in spreading the teachings of another."

Without knowledge and understanding of Scripture we can't adequately accomplish this aspect of discipleship.

Capturing the Word is so much more than simply reading the Bible. Students can't grow if their only interaction with the Word of God comes during a message. We cannot produce hearers of the Word only, but we must also make doers (James 1.22).

> *A disciple is one who embraces and assists in spreading the teachings of another.*

Here are a few more suggestions:

Give students a verse to memorize each week. Imagine a new

sixth grade student entering your youth ministry and remaining through graduation. If they memorize just one new verse a week, they would have memorized over 350 verses! Now think of what that may mean for a graduate entering college, a job, and adult church.

Have students read a portion of Scripture until they come to a verse they can apply to their life. Rather than read a chapter and forget what they read, have them read, looking for the application of what they are reading. They may only read a few verses that day but they will walk away with a clear application for their life.

Have students write down a couple of sentences from the passage they just read.

Help students secure a Bible app on their phone. They can follow one of the many reading plans set up specifically for students.

Using a Bible app, have students listen to the Bible on their phones as they drive/ride to school, while they get ready for school, or while they prepare for bed.

One of the most helpful things I did as a new follower was to highlight, underline and write notes in my Bible. Believe it or not, many students have never thought of this.

Communicate

Empower students to communicate their journey with Jesus to others.

Empowering students to share their faith is both necessary and rewarding for a follower.

I can't begin to describe the joy my daughter, Lindsay had when she gave birth to a son. What I didn't fully realize was the great joy I felt when my daughter gave birth. Tears filled my eyes as I realized new birth through someone I had helped bring into this world.

How much more in a spiritual sense! Engaging students in evangelism, having them spiritually reproduce another life, ignites their faith and develops maturity in their walk with the Lord. It also makes you a spiritual grandparent, which is pretty cool too.

Create a Culture of Reproducers

Philemon 6 – "…and I pray that the sharing of your faith may become effective for the full knowledge of every good thing that is in us for the sake of Christ." (ESV)

Paul prays that in the sharing of our faith we may have the full knowledge of every good thing in us for Christ! Not only do others hear the gospel but we benefit by realizing who we are in Christ.

We've seen or heard it before but if you began your youth ministry with just one disciple and he/she reproduced themselves just once in six months, and each new disciple did the same, in just four years you'd have 256 *reproducing* disciples.

Remember, great things always begin small in the Kingdom.

Here's an easy way for students to communicate their relationship with Jesus. Have students write out or share with another student the following:

What my life was like prior to meeting Jesus.

How did I hear about Jesus?

Why did I decide to receive Jesus as my Savior?

How has my life been different as a result?

Another way a teen can communicate their faith in Christ is to be baptized in Water. Water baptism is not only a command from our Lord but is paramount to our growth and brings about identification with our Savior.

Have a water baptism service for students at a time when family and friends are able to be present. Consider making this a way to reach parents and families who don't attend your church by holding it at a pool or lake. Each teen gives a short testimony of why they are being baptized. Take a picture to give to the student later as a reminder of their commitment. Have a BBQ following so you can connect with parents.

If you've been on a mission trip, then you know there is nothing like it! It builds faith in students, as they believe God for the necessary finances for the trip. It creates a level of discipline as students prepare for the trip and as their ability to be flexible is challenged on the foreign field.

Many students are involved in campus clubs thus giving them opportunity to communicate their faith on a regular basis.

Here's a testimony from a young girl regarding her campus club experience.

"These past couple of weeks have been awesome! This year I have really stepped out in my school to love and notice everyone around me! Two Wednesdays ago I invited a couple of my friends who don't know Jesus to come to church with me because we were having a big event and they came and all accepted Christ as their Savior! I gave them each a Bible to read and dig deeper into the word! I am also starting a campus club at my school, we have been doing Wednesday mornings but tomorrow is our first day doing it every Friday! I am excited to see what God has planned for this year!"

Contribute

Every year I challenged my students to give $100 and raise $100 for missions. This was the norm for us as a youth group. Each week we challenged our students to give two dollars toward their goal. Challenging your students to only give money they raised toward missions creates the wrong culture.

Leaders must task students to personally give toward the cause of Christ.

Create a Culture of Contributors.

As a disciple I am able to contribute in a variety of ways. I can give my life, resources, gifts, future, decisions…everything to him. I make it my goal to grow in serving and giving.

We may never be more like Jesus than when we are serving others. Imagine the change of culture in your youth ministry as students learn to serve on the campus, in their community and church.

As with all the disciplines, this must be learned. Serving doesn't come naturally but is developed as we take time with our students, modeling a servant's heart. If we truly want to create great students we must build servants. Jesus said to be great in God's Kingdom is to be the servant of all. (Matthew 20.26) Who doesn't want great students?

A few ideas:

Do a chore at home each day without being asked

Volunteer to serve on their campus.

Gather students to serve at a shelter or food pantry.

Challenge students to sacrificially give to missions.

Have students come early to help set up for the service.

Hold a free car wash for the community.

Clean a neighborhood block or city park.

Students volunteer to serve in another area of the church.

Do yard work for a neighbor.

Volunteer to vacuum and/or wash their parent's car.

Babysit for free for a young couple who can't afford to pay.

One particular Saturday we got the whole youth group together to paint a single mom's house. I was so proud of our group as we painted the entire exterior in just one afternoon. Our students loved the creative way to serve and the single mom bragged to the church about those incredible teenagers!

Try to balance what and how you serve between the campus, community and church. Tell the story of how your teens gave to your pastor and the adults in your congregation. This helps to change the perception that adults have that teens are animals, monsters and aliens.

It's the lecture-lab, audio-visual-tactile, theology-disciplines-experiences, all wrapped up into one. It's synergistic in its approach, developing core training, periods of stretching, and great intensity.

CULTURE SHAPING QUESTIONS:

What are some ways you can help students connect with God?

What are some ways you can engage your students in capturing God's Word in their life?

What are some ways you can empower students to communicate their faith to others?

What are some ways you can encourage your students to contribute?

FOURTEEN

CULTURE CONNECTORS

In the previous chapter I shared ideas for individual students. In this chapter I want to look at cultural connections for your entire youth ministry.

Empowering students for ministry demands four major connections are made. The four connections are as follows: Youth ministries must have a connection with God, the family, the Church, and Christ's Cause. For any one of these to be missing jeopardizes the stamina and effectiveness of the student.

To ensure that each student is properly connected, the youth leader must provide necessary power supplies. The last thing we want to do as leaders is attempt to plug a student into the proper outlets, only to find out that we fell short in our connections.

Extension cords and adapters allow us to connect appliances with a power source, thus equipping them to accomplish the task at hand. Ideally, having students as close to the source of power is optimal, but at times making these vital connections will require extending ourselves to reach them. Because every student is not the same we will need adapters in our arsenal to then be able to help students plug in. Let's take a look.

Once you've read this chapter, do the exercise at the end to determine how well you're currently connecting teens and what areas you might need to focus on in the coming weeks.

Connected to God

Generally speaking, as youth leaders we are pretty good at connecting our students to God. We do this through our worship services, our messages, response times, service projects, camps, various activities, etc…

Worship is a primary ingredient to building a disciple into a life-long follower of Christ. Worship is so much more than singing songs. Sure, it's the most common way we worship our Lord, but worship involves a deep commitment and obedience to God's Word.

1 Samuel 15.22 "But Samuel replied: 'Does the Lord delight in burnt offerings and sacrifices as much as in obeying the voice of the Lord? To obey is better than sacrifice, and to heed is better than the fat of rams.'" (NIV. Emphasis mine.)

Worship is about obedience to God's Word. It's about placing Jesus first in our daily decisions. We worship God best when we obey God most.

Someone once said, "What you love you worship, what you worship you serve." Leading your teens into a lifestyle of worship eventually determines what or who they will serve. It becomes crucial that we connect our teens with our Savior through worship.

Create a culture of worship

> *Worship is about obedience to God's Word. It's about placing Jesus first in our daily decisions. We worship God best when we obey God most.*

Connected to Family

Before discussing this, take a moment to define 'family' in your own words. What comes to mind when you think of family?

God's design for the home is that of a father, mother and children. Unfortunately, this definition is no longer the norm. Several circumstances have changed the face of the home and as a result, we are left ministering to students from a multitude of family backgrounds.

Consider your own youth ministry. If your ministry is like most you have students who have had multiple fathers or mothers, come from divorced homes, are adopted or in foster care, have never met their biological parent, come from a single parent home, have step-brothers/sisters, blended families, live with their grandparents or other relatives…the list goes on.

A quick look at a few examples from Scripture reveals similar breakdowns in the home.

> Abraham, Sarah and Hagar
> Jacob, Leah and Rachel
> Hosea and Gomer
> David, Bathsheba and Solomon
> Naomi and Ruth
> Moses, his mother, Jochebed, and Pharaoh's' daughter

Even Jesus had stepbrothers.

God has not simply called us to teens, but we are also called to the families these teens find themselves in. We have the incredible privilege of embracing entire families for the Kingdom.

Create a Culture of Family

One thing that has changed drastically in homes over the past several years is how few families actually sit down and interact. The dinner table has changed drastically. No longer do families enjoy a meal together, laughing, sharing and discussing the events of the day.

Small groups become that connection point for the family of God. Sharing a meal or snacks, praying together, singing a song and discussing the Scriptures all are a part of a healthy youth ministry. Small groups connect your students as a family.

Here are a few more ideas for connecting families:

Invite all parents to a special dinner. Here they will experience their son/daughter in some sort of arts presentation and hear a bit more about what happens in the youth ministry. Students can sing, do drama, play an instrument, lead in a song of worship, recite a poem, etc… Consider doing this at their son/daughter's school or other public meeting place outside the church.

This will further help break down parent's reservations in believing you are only trying to get them to come to your church. It's all about their teenager and starting to build a relationship with them.

Greet the entire family, not just the student.

Text, email, call or drop a note on parent's birthdays, anniversaries, job promotions, etc… This lets the parent know that you genuinely care about them and not just their teen.

Consider having a greeter welcome each parent as they drop their teen off for youth group. The greeter can give them information regarding upcoming events, express thanks, and even occasionally hand out a snack and/or beverage as a way to show appreciation to the parent/guardian for dropping off their teens.

Have a parent's social media page. In addition to giving details of upcoming events, give article links for parenting helps, encouraging words, brag about teens in your ministry, brag about parents, and invitations to special events.

One way we made our youth ministry more alluring to our parents was to hold distinctive events to connect teens and parents. We did several progressive dinners, visiting 3-4 homes during the dinner.

Some parents prepared meals, others hosted the teens, and others drove teens from home to home. Get as many parents involved as possible. If your youth group is too large for an activity such as a progressive dinner, do the event as a small group or only for seniors or only for grades 6-8.

Some more ideas:

Hold a free car wash for the community and make sure you invite all your parents.

Deliver fresh baked goods/plants/flowers to parents while they are at work.

Have a Parent's Sundae. Have the students serve ice cream with all the toppings to parents following an activity. Gives parents a chance to hang out following one of your events.

Host a "preparing for college night" for Juniors and Seniors and their parents. Have an admissions director from one of the local colleges help prepare everyone for this transition.

Send out a survey to your parents regarding your youth ministry. Ask key questions to help you in planning for the future. Offer a dinner out to someone who completes the survey as incentive. You can find easy on-line survey tools to help you with this.

Do a service project for one of the single parents in your youth ministry.

Collect food or an offering for a family going through a financial struggle.

Visit a parent while in the hospital.

Get to know the brothers and sisters of the teens in your youth group.

Finally, make sure you know the parent's (guardians) name so when you see them in church or at an activity you can address them by name.

What other ideas come to mind in connecting parents and teens?

Connected to Church

It's extremely important to realize that our ministry to teens is not to simply raise better teenagers. We are also called to build better adult disciples. In just a few short years many, if not most of them will be leaving for college or a job. Regardless of the reasons, some will need or want to change churches in the next couple of years. It behooves us to make this transition easier through connection to the larger body of Christ.

We have an incredible opportunity as youth leaders to shape the course of church life by equipping and empowering teens while in our youth ministries. In addition to becoming leaders in our youth ministries, many students will become future leaders in churches.

Let's not forget that even Jesus had a transition plan in place. Once he left the disciples, he gave them the Holy Spirit to help them in the next phase of life and ministry. He knew the disciples would need a helper during transition and beyond.

Here are a few ideas for connecting students to the Church.

Get students involved in other ministries outside of youth. Many of your teens could serve in children's church, as an usher, in the sound booth, with the worship ministry, with Sunday School, etc… Work with the other ministry departments and brainstorm on how to make this happen.

Make sure you get your students to camps, conventions, and statewide or regional activities. My kids all loved seeing their friends and adult leaders from across the state during these times. It reminded them they were a part of something much bigger.

It's true some teens cease from attending church once they graduate high school. This doesn't mean they left the faith, however. There are many reasons for a drop-off at this transitional point. I'm not suggesting that everyone falls within these categories, but let's not assume that simply because a teen is not in church on a Sunday following graduation that they've turned their back on Christ.

Here are just a few reasons we may see less college-aged students in our churches:

They are attending a Christian college in another city. They attend chapel each day, don't have a vehicle to get to church, or consider their chapel attendance their church.

A student moves to another city, and for a variety of reasons, is unable to find a church in town, thus they are no longer 'counted' as attending church.

A student moves to another city and has a difficult time making relationships with people in the church.

Church is seen as more of an event a student attends rather than a meaningful, faith-building experience. Once out of the house they choose to attend the 'event' when convenient rather than as an aspect of their growing faith in Christ.

They never learned to practice good time management and as a result, they find the increased pressure of college and/or job takes away from attending church.

A student gets a job that requires them to work some/all Sundays.

They no longer live under the rules of their parents' regarding church attendance. They go through a period of faith discovery on their own.

Understand I'm not suggesting these are good excuses for not attending church. Rather, my hope is that while they're in our youth ministries, we can address some of these and help teens make a strong connection to the church. Talk with teens about their transition and help them make a plan on how they can remain connected. Making such a connection helps teens remain faithful to the body of Christ long after graduation.

Our responsibility as leaders is to follow up with every graduating student until we've done all we can to connect them with a body of believers. So rather than criticize youth ministry for seemingly doing a poor job, let's strategize on how to ensure that students remain connected.

1 Peter 5.2 – "Care for the flock that God has entrusted to you. Watch over it willingly, not grudgingly—not for what you will get out of it, but because you are eager to serve God." (NLT)

Here's how we can help students stay connected.

Find out what city a student is moving to and contact a good church in town. Give them information regarding the student and ask the church to follow up on them. Every so often make contact with the church and student.

Follow each graduating student through the variety of social networking sites to ensure that each student has found a church.

If a student remains in the area, help them get involved in a ministry and/or group within the church. Consider them as a volunteer leader in your youth ministry.

Visit former students at their place of employment or occasionally take them to lunch or meet for coffee.

Assign incoming seniors with one or two graduates to follow up. This provides the follow up for the graduate, gives leadership to seniors and lets them know that they will have a form of accountability once they graduate.

These are just a few ways to help students connect. Keep in mind we are not to simply pastor students during the seven years within our immediate care: we are to pastor them through times of transitions.

Connected to Christ's Cause

If you've been in youth ministry for any length of time at all then you've heard the question, "What is God's will (purpose/cause/mission) for my life?"

The quick answer is that we are ALL called to serve as ministers of the gospel.

As youth leaders we have the joy of making a significant impact on a teen's future. Of course it is God who calls, but we have a unique role of confirming this call and then challenging them to carry the good news to the next generation.

Looking back, I now see the numerous confirmations to God's call on my life. These confirmations came from my youth pastor and other leaders in the in the youth ministry. It was the constant reminders of God's call from others that led me to where I am today.

Never underestimate the power of your words as a youth leader in the life of a student. The words you speak today continue to echo in the hearts of students throughout their life.

One way to ensure students get connected to Christ's cause is to assemble events and outings that give students a broad range of experiences.

Here are a few ideas.

Engage students in several of the ministries within the church. One way of approaching this is to put a rotating schedule in place so each student can participate. Perhaps one Sunday a month a student experiences a new church ministry in which to serve.

These can include: parking lot attendant, greeter, usher, nursery worker, children church, media ministry, worship team, serve coffee, etc... The idea is to expose them to multiple opportunities over the course of their time in your youth ministry.

Lead a campus club or small group.

Each week pray as a group for a specific group of workers. This could include people in church ministry, workers at the local mall, restaurant workers, doctors, stay-at-home moms, missionaries, teachers, actors, and so on. Doing so brings a value to each area of employment.

Challenge students to give sacrificially to missions. As an example, consider a six-week long period where students are asked to give to a specific mission.

Provide opportunities for students to speak, receive the offering, lead an activity, and be a part of worship within your youth ministry.

Encourage students to get involved in the arts at school or in your community. Consider a drama ministry at your church as well.

Host a 'job fair' for students. Invite individuals from your church to share what they do for a living and how they live out their faith in the workplace. Make it a three-hour event on a Saturday morning, giving each individual 15 minutes to share and field questions. Provide coffee/bagels at the beginning and/or lunch at the end.

Periodically share that God calls each of us as followers no matter our vocation. His cause or mission is to be expressed in every arena of life. Whether a student is called to be a stay at home parent, a minister, a factory worker, a missionary, a teacher, a hairdresser, etc... we are all called to the cause of Christ.

Gear a weekend retreat around knowing and following God's call in your life.

Every student experiences a cross-cultural missions experience prior to graduation.

Engage students in community projects. This may include doing projects for the city such as painting fire hydrants, street cleaning, sign painting, cleaning a city park, etc... This sparks a servant attitude in the hearts of students and teaches them that the church is to serve the community rather than the other way around.

Challenge students to give a year of their life to a cause following graduation. There are many opportunities available for service. Several organizations even offer college credit while engaging in their mission.

> *One way to ensure students get connected to Christ's cause is to assemble events and outings that give students a broad range of experiences.*

Let's remember that your culture is defined by the language, attitudes, experiences, behaviors, facility, and décor of your group. Each of these along with your programs, events, and services need to reflect the culture you are creating.

Take a moment to do the following exercise. This gives you a good idea of the strengths and areas to improve on in your youth ministry.

Record every event, service and activity you do in a year around the box. What events, services and activities connect you to God, Parents, Church and Christ's Cause?

For example, you may write 'annual mission trip' on the Christ's Cause side of the box. 'Youth retreat' may appear next to the God side of the box.

Once you recorded each event, including church-wide events and activities, you'll have a good idea of what connections you are making and which connections need to be emphasized.

Try to place each activity on only one side of the box. Some may be able to be placed at more than one but start by placing them on the side that has the greatest connection.

God

Cause   Family

Church

CULTURE SHAPING QUESTIONS:

Give five ways you are connecting students to God.

What are a few benefits to connecting students to family?

What long-term value is there in connecting students to the Church?

What are some church-wide events, services and activities you can engage your students in to help connect them to the Church?

Why is it important we connect students to Christ's cause?

FIFTEEN

KEEPING IT REAL

It's my prayer that this book has been helpful to you in your efforts to create culture. I remind you that creating culture does not happen overnight. It takes time to develop the culture you wish to establish.

I've learned the following principles over the past 30 plus years of youth ministry that have helped me create culture. My hope is that the following will help you as you create culture.

Be A Disciple That Prays And Studies God's Word.

Avoid the temptation to create culture on your own merits. Allow the Holy Spirit to speak to you in these times of prayer and study of Scripture. What you'll find is the Spirit will direct your paths as you spend time in God's presence.

Be A Great Leader by Being a Great Follower.

Let's remember that we began this journey as followers. God increases your level of influence as you faithfully follow. Want to reach more teens? Allow God to reach more of you.

Begin By Creating A Healthy Culture In Your Home.

Your ministry assignment may change several times over the course of your life. Your family is forever. Students today need to see healthy families in order to establish their own healthy family. Remember, your goal is not better 14-year-old students. Your aim is better 40-year-old followers.

Make Sure Your Private Life And Your Public Life Match.

I want people to say I lived what I preached. Rather than ask your spouse or close friend if the message was good, ask them if you're living out what you just spoke.

Continue Growing In Your Relationship With Christ.

Perhaps this goes without saying, but I've seen too many individuals let the stage of success define their relationship with Christ. Guard and grow your walk with Christ above all things. This is what being a disciple is all about.

Create a Culture of Discipleship

Take a moment and write out your prayer, plan, and process to be a disciple who makes disciples.

Devotional Resource for Your Students

Help your students walk with power. PowerWalk is a yearlong, journal-devotional, geared to daily engage students with Christ.

Why?

Because walking with Jesus has more to do with devotion than having devotions. I've written a student devotional with this very purpose in mind. It allows both the creative and disciplined side to burst forth as they love God with their heart, soul, mind and strength.

PowerWalking

...races you through 192 captivating stories from the Bible. Why? Because the Bible is a story about God and because everyone loves stories! Each quarter (13 weeks) you'll read and walk through 48 stories from Scripture.

...speeds you up if you fall behind. Life gets crazy for each of us. It allows time to catch up for those days/weeks when we are extra busy. Each week has two days (Sunday and Wednesday) and each quarter (13th week) a full week to catch up. Of course, there is no completion deadline. Just do your best to walk with Jesus each day.

...stretches your creativity as you express your devotion to God. No two people are the same. PowerWalk appeals to your imagination and desire to walk closer with Jesus. You'll read fascinating stories, have opportunity to express your feelings, illustrate scenes, interact with the story and be challenged to live out the stories you just read.

...exercises the disciplines of Scripture reading, prayer, worship, journaling, memorization of Scripture, and note taking.

...walks you through the Bible on a chronological path. That's a fancy way for saying the stories are in the order they happened. So as your story unfolds, you're reading how God's story developed and continues today.

Go to RodWhitlock.com to order!

NOTES

Made in the USA
San Bernardino, CA
19 May 2016